All Plants Are Edible Once

CHRIS DINESEN ROGERS

DEDICATION

To Norm

CONTENTS

ACKNOWLEDGMENTS

To all of the herbalists, folklore practitioners, and common people who shared their knowledge and wisdom. I thank you.

1 FOLKLORE AND PLANTS

Imagine a time where there were no corner drugstores. You couldn't get bandages for a simple cut or the antibiotic ointment to keep it from getting infected. Heaven forbid you should come down with a cough or cold. Tummy feeling upset? Hope you feel better soon.

Back in the day, wild plants were your pharmacy. They cured your ailments, soothed your wounds, and calmed your nerves. Those who understood their uses were revered for their knowledge. As Hippocrates, the father of medicine, once said, "*Let food be thy medicine, and medicine be thy food.*"

Ironically, many foods that once were considered wild edible plants have made their way into grocery stores. Foods like dandelion, purslane, and echinacea are all common plants that you can find in your grocery store's produce section or at your pharmacy.

The Doctrine of Signatures

The starting point for understanding modern uses of edible and medicinal plants comes from a 15th century philosophy called the Doctrine of Signatures. German mystic, Jakob Böhme, wrote of the premise in his book, *The Signature of All Things*. Swiss philosopher, Philippus von Hohenheim also known as Paracelsus, espoused the belief as well. The premise was simple. God provided all one needed to know. All you had to do was study the visual clues He left.

For example, bloodroot, a common spring wildflower, has bright orange-red sap. Therefore, it must be the cure for blood disorders. The leaves of hepatica, another spring wildflower, resemble the liver. Therefore, it must be sign from God that it was the plant to seek a cure for liver ailments. Paracelsus, ironically, is also known as the father of toxicology.

The Doctrine of Signatures was widely practiced during its day. It provided the names of many common plants, such as toothwort, wormwood, and ginseng. Today, the Doctrine of Signatures is viewed more like superstition than true science. However, it pays to note the characteristics of a plant, if just to help identify it.

Longest Running Medical Study

Folklore medicine depended upon observation. You can think of it as the longest running medical study ever. If the catnip tea helped the baby sleep, it must the perfect cure for a fussy child. If eating peppermint leaves soothed your stomach, it is a certain cure for digestive ailments.

All plants, after all, possessed a spirit for good or bad. They could treat other types of ills, such as the dispelling the evil eye or removing a hex. Some plants could invite good luck or provide a means for getting rid of an enemy or rival.

While the ancient Greeks and Romans associated plants with gods and goddesses, people of the Middle Ages saw some plants as agents of the devil. The prickly pear cactus, otherwise known as devil's tongue, is a good example. One look at it, and you can easily surmise the premise.

In a world where so much was unknown, the lore of plants offered some solace. Observations of the effects of some plants gave them almost a miraculous quality. The appearance of medicinal plants that could cure it in the spring may have inspired some of the associations of it being a time of renewal.

Sorrel and dandelion, both excellent sources of vitamin C, magically cured someone suffering from the effects of scurvy, a serious nutrient deficiency. Scurvy causes a range of symptoms from loss of appetite to shortness of breath to gum disease. It affected many sea explorers of the Renaissance era.

A cure of this malady first came in 1536 by a French explorer named Jacques Cartier. Cartier learned from the Iroquois that a concoction of needles of an evergreen mixed with hot water could provide relief. Cartier's crew recovered thanks to the nutritional properties of this so-called "*tree of life*"; we know it as arborvitae.

Stories of the cures and culinary delights became part of the folklore of wild plants, passed from generation to generation. The ones with the strongest evidence persisted and prompted closer scrutiny later by the scientific community.

Verified Medicinal Uses

Many folklore uses of wild plants have been verified by scientific research. Perhaps one of the most common is acetylsalicylic acid or simply, aspirin. Salicylic acid is a plant extract found in willow trees. Its use as an analgesic goes back to the time of Hippocrates in 400 BC.

Herbalists used it to relieve pain and discomfort from colds and fevers. The folklore said willows could even provide protection against sorcery and the evil eye. In 1853, a French chemist named Charles Frederic Gerhardt synthesized what would later become aspirin.

This isn't the only proven medicinal use of a wild plant. Echinacea has also shown to reduce the incidence of colds, earaches, and sinusitis, confirming its use by American Indians and by herbalists as we know from the folklore. Numerous other examples exist including:

- Dandelion
- Nettle
- Ginseng
- Mullein
- Peppermint

In fact, about 40 percent of the drugs used in the Western world are derived from plants that have had a long history of folklore use. Some estimates put it up to 80 percent. And we thought it was just the rain forests with their bounty of untapped potential. It exists right outside your window.

Folklore and Lost Stories

One of the more enjoyable aspects of collecting wild edible and medicinal plants are the stories associated with the plants and how they were named. With some plants, such as feverfew, you have a pretty good idea what it was used for historically.

Other plants, such as boneset, may leave you scratching your head. Boneset, as it turns out, was used by the Confederates during the Civil War as a substitute for quinine for treating fevers in the field.

Some plants may make you chuckle, like burdock, otherwise known as "*love leaf.*" An old husband's tale says that eating the stems would "*stir up lust.*" And others intrigue us, with questions and musings, like what in the world is swine's snout?

With this preamble, let us begin our journey of the wild edible and medicinal plants. Prepare yourself for some surprises. Pour yourself a cuppa of pine needle tea and pull up a chair. Let's find out just what is five fingers.

2 FIRST THINGS FIRST

The Basics of Collecting

First things first. You cannot just go collecting plants and start making dinner. Maybe you could, but you may run into a couple of problems, such as getting ticketed or even worse, getting poisoned. Neither makes for a good experience, so let's go over what you should and should not do.

Legal Collection

Just because you are on public lands to do your collecting, it does not mean that it is a permissible activity. Some sites may restrict all harvesting. Others may prohibit certain plants, such as ginseng or goldenseal. Others may require permits. It always pays to check.

A lot depends upon the type of plant and what parts you are collecting. Berries, mushrooms, and other fruits come back the following year. Pulling up roots destroys the entire plant, making the former okay in some areas and the latter, not.

The habitat itself may be another reason. Some plants may grow in the same habitat as threatened or endangered plants. They may grow near plants that are often poached, such as rare orchids.

Trashing around in wetlands will likely do a lot of ecological damage. Your first task, therefore, is to check if collecting is legal and permitted **where** you want to collect. You'll save yourself a truckload of hassle with one phone call.

Private lands are another matter. Trespassing is trespassing whether you are just walking the property or harvesting wild plants. Sometimes the land will be posted, so you at least have an idea of the attitude of the landowner about visitors on his property. Heed the warning; not all states require signage in order to claim trespassing, however.

Timing of Collection

Public lands serve multiple needs. Some uses trump others during certain times of the year. You may find that some sites ban visitor traffic during hunting seasons. Others may restrict access during bird breeding seasons or migration. Usually these types of closures are well-advertised, if just for the sign at the park entrance that states "No Visitor Traffic. Hunting In Progress."

If a site has a restoration plan for an area, it may be closed for management such as prescribed burns. With these cases, you can't blame the site manager. As a former natural resources employee, I can vouch for the fact that site managers may not have the luxury of knowing too far in advance if a burn is going to happen. Conditions have to be just so. All of this is tested on the day of the event before a call is made.

Pesticide Use and Other Contaminants

Some edible and medicinal plants may even be found in city parks. Chemicals used to keep pests under control present a problem at the site and nearby. Pesticide drift may contaminate areas adjacent to actively managed sites. This unfortunate occurrence may also apply to roadsides, abandoned farm fields, and other like sites.

Contaminants don't just apply to pesticides. Urban runoff from roads and parking lots can contain a wide variety of toxins that would render a harmless plant dangerous to consume. They can do anything from give you a nasty belly ache to something much worse.

Some common pesticides used for agriculture are carcinogens. Others can cause birth defects and other health issues from long-term exposure. With perennial plants, the risk exists that contaminants can accumulate in the plant's tissues. You will have to assume the role of food inspector and vet all of your specimens well.

You will find several plants listed as noxious weeds, either by state or federal standards. I've indicated this status where known in the plant description. That means that the plant is considered invasive and therefore, is illegal to plant or sell in that area. It's worth noting this information because in those particular areas, these plants may be routinely sprayed—along with any plants you want to collect in the immediate vicinity.

While all of this may seem like overkill, remember that eating or using some wild plants carries risks. Your goal is to minimize the ones that you can control, like where you collect and the proper identification. As my college botany professor once said, "*All plants are edible once.*" You want to enjoy the good ones again, don't you? Our friend, Paracelsus, offered some more advice when he said, "*The dose makes the poison.*" This leads to my 10 Rules of Collecting Wild Plants:

1. Make sure it's legal to collect at your site, and it is not protected by state or federal law

2. Verify that pesticides haven't been applied (as best as you can determine)

3. Avoid areas in the path of urban or agricultural runoff

4. Know how to identify poisonous plants

5. Know the right time of year to collect

6. Know what parts of the plant can be safely used

7. Only try a little of a plant before a lot

8. People with allergies should avoid contact with plants in the Daisy Family

9. Pay attention to habitat and season

And most importantly,

10. **Be absolutely and totally positive of your identification**

Plants of the Same Genus

Some plant families contain species that are both edible and poisonous. The Parsley Family is a good example. This group contains the caraway, similar to what you can get at the grocery store. The family also includes poison hemlock, a plant that is deadly if consumed. Socrates would know.

This is an example where paying close attention to all identifying characteristics is vital. Caraway smells, well, like caraway. Poison hemlock, on the other hand, has a foul scent when the leaves are crushed. Don't be fooled, however. There is a very good reason why poison is in its name. You should also avoid contact with poison hemlock juice as it is toxic and may cause dermatitis.

Sap, Hairs, and Thorns, Oh My!

Sap, hairs, and thorns are the nuisances you will encounter with collecting wild plants. The sap of many plants may cause contact dermatitis. The hairs of plants like nettle, for example, can cause a painful burning sensation.

While they may hamper the collection, hairs don't get in the way of enjoying nettle as an edible plant. Dried plants do not sting. The thing to remember is that it's not just the plants that you collect, but the ones nearby, with stinging nettle being the notable one here. If you're collecting in bottomlands, you better know how to identify stinging nettle.

Another concern may surprise you. A lesser known type of hazard involves plants that can cause photodermatitis, such as cow parsnip. This irritating condition occurs when you are exposed to sunlight after contact with the plant. It will cause an itchy red rash not unlike poison ivy. A good field guide will alert you to these dangers.

Hay Fever Sufferers, Beware!

If you suffer from hay fever, you need to be careful about certain plants. Ragweed is in the Aster or Daisy Family of plants. This large family includes many common varieties such as compass plant, chicory, and sunflower as well as several plants included in this collection like aster and purple coneflower.

Because other plants are related genetically, a risk exists that they may cause a similar reaction in you. Your field guide will undoubtedly tell you what family a particular plant is from. If it says aster, composite, sunflower, or daisy, approach any species with caution. On the plus side, in a way, you should know right away if the plant will bother you. That particular immune response tends to be swift.

100 Percent Edible—Not!

Just because you can eat one part of a plant does not mean that the entire plant is edible. Take rhubarb, for example. The stalks are tasty however you prepare them. Just be sure not to eat the leaves. They contain a poison called oxalic acid that can damage your kidneys.

Another thing to bear in mind concerns wildlife. Just because animals eat certain plants doesn't mean you can too. Turkeys, for example, will munch on poison ivy berries during the winter. As they say in the car commercials, don't try this at home.

The same dangers lurk with other plants, such as cherries and apples. The fruits are fine to eat, of course. The seeds and pits, though, contain cyanide. It's important, therefore, to get the whole story about the wild plants before you eat anything.

Drug Interactions

If you're taking any kind of prescription drug, you're probably aware that you have to vet everything else you take to prevent harmful drug interactions. This precaution includes any supplements, over-the-counter medications, and sometimes, even foods that you eat. The same advice apply to wild plants.

The reasons vary. Some plants may have the same effect as the medications you're taking. For example, if you're taking a diuretic for high blood pressure, you should use caution eating dandelion because of its similar properties. This can throw off the dosage of the drugs you're taking and in some cases, lead to overdosing or under-dosing with others.

Other wild plants may interfere with the actions of your prescription and therefore, make them ineffective. Others may worsen pre-existing conditions, such as echinacea for persons with lupus, multiple sclerosis, and other autoimmune disorders. If in doubt, ask your doctor. Put another way, if in doubt, leave it out.

All plants contain hundreds of chemicals. Some apple varieties, for example, have over 350 volatile compounds in them. They include unexpected ones, such as ethanol, camphor, and propanol. Don't forget about the cyanide in the seeds, formaldehyde, and acetone. Then, there is also tricosene, an insect pheromone used in pesticides.

My point in bringing this up is to remind you that natural items consist of chemicals—lots of them. This means that unknown substances can carry a risk of drug interactions with anything you take. Most of the plants contained in this book are similar to common edible varieties, so chances are you wouldn't be exposed to too many new substances. Just be smart if you take prescription or over-the-counter medications for an existing health condition.

Mushrooms

Mushrooms are a special case. Most times if you eat the wrong one, you don't just get sick, you get really, really sick. Some can even kill you. I would not advise collecting mushrooms maybe with only one exception, morels. Even morels carry one caution, however.

There is a similar species called the false morel that you don't want to eat. The good morels grow in the spring. The bad one grows at other times of the year. They look similar though there are key differences.

The morel is hollow and trumpet-shaped, whereas, the false morel looks more like a brain with convolutions rather than pits. Time of the year, therefore, is very important with mushroom identification.

Plant Identification and Collection

Several tools will help you correctly identify plants and safely collect them. A fanny pack with a pouch for a water bottle can hold everything you need. One of the most important tools of the trade is a small magnifying glass or loupe for confirming identification of wild plants. It can be helpful for determining things like if a stem is hairless or grooved.

A pruning shears is invaluable for collecting plants with woody or thick stems. You should also carry a pair of garden gloves, insect spray, and a mini first-aid kit. I use one when we go geocaching. I keep a few band-aids, some moleskin, antibiotic ointment, and ibuprofen along for all of our ventures.

If you are allergic to poison ivy or have allergies, you should take along some antihistamine and cortisone cream in case you encounter something you shouldn't. You might also try a barrier cream against poison ivy. The plant is so widespread that it is hard to avoid it in most collecting situations. You're better off to be prepared than to suffer the consequences—also take special note of the chapter on jewelweed.

For wild plants, I'd recommend both paper bags and plastic bags. Paper does well with plants that may get moldy. Plastic bags are good for plant parts like nuts and berries. Take along a marker to for noting what you've collected and where. You might also want to create a map with waypoints for the good collecting sites on your smartphone. Androids apps like ViewRanger GPS can come in handy for this task.

To round up your tools, of course, you should have your field guide. A notebook is a good idea as well. I use a for keeping notes of where I've found plants so I know where to come back to next year. An alternative is a smartphone note taking app, such as the Evernote. You can take geo-tagged photos to make the tracking next year easier.

About the Plants

I chose the plants included in this book for several reasons. Many of them have fascinating stories and folklore use. The irony is that some of the most common plants around us have the most interesting past. This is especially so of the maligned ones like dandelion and creeping Charlie. Being a weed doesn't not exempt these plants from being the subject of a good old husband's tale or two.

Other plants have a personal connection or story, like jewelweed. One day, my sister, her son, and I were walking a nature path running along a stream. He was maybe six or seven at the time. Unfortunately, he brushed against some stinging nettle. The patch he happened upon was especially virulent being as it was spring. Fortunately, as luck would have it, jewelweed was also growing nearby.

I knew what to do. I plucked a plant and rubbed its sap on the affected area. I don't think Brian was expecting it to act so quickly at the time. My sister remarked how she enjoyed this granola moment. I had to include jewelweed.

This book is by no means a comprehensive list of the plants with a history of medicinal or culinary use. The list is endless. These are just my personal favorites from my own study of plants that I've researched through the years. I hope you enjoy the stories. And maybe you might think a little differently before you pull that yarrow out of your garden.

Because I'm from the Midwest, the plants reflect that perspective. I don't have anything against Southern species or those found out West. I'm a Midwest girl who has extensive experience with these plants only.

Disclaimer:

The contents of this book are meant for educational purposes only. It is not intended to be a substitute or adjunct to medical advice.

The author has attempted to research this topic to its fullest, but does not accept any responsibility for consequences from collecting, using, or ingesting any of the wild plants mentioned.

It is the responsibility of the individual to properly identify all plants and exercise caution prior to, during, and following collection. All readers are strongly encouraged to contact their doctors before adding new supplements or foods to their diet.

On another note, many historical uses may baffle us today. Some may even offend. I'm only the messenger, reading the news. The references to ugly women, "*female problems*," or lack of libido are not my own. I include them so you can know the stories about the plants including the good, bad, and the politically incorrect. As the late Jennifer Patterson once said, "If you don't want to know the truth, look away."

Without further ado, on to the plants!

3 ANGELICA

Common name: Angelica

Other names: Great angelica, masterwort, American angelica, purple angelica, bellyache root, scurvy pea

Scientific name: *Angelica atropurpurea*, Carrot Family

Habitat: Wet forests and meadows, stream banks

Season: Summer

Status: Native

Type: Perennial forb

Identifying characteristics: White or greenish-white umbels; stems are thick and reddish, not unlike rhubarb

Edible parts: Root, stem, and leaf

Special cautions: If you're pregnant, don't use angelica. It can stimulate menstrual flow. There are other precautions too. The plant may cause photodermatitis or sun poisoning. Exposure to UV light—especially the midday sun—causes itchy bumps and rashes in some individuals, not unlike a really bad case of poison ivy.

If you collect angelica, make sure you have the right one. And pay attention when collecting it. Angelica prefers the same habitat as species you don't want to stumble upon, including poison hemlock and stinging nettle. Related species are threatened or endangered in Maryland, Rhode Island, and Tennessee.

Folklore

Much of the folklore surrounding angelica comes from another species in this genus called *Angelica archangelica* or garden angelica. Some texts also refer to it as Norwegian angelica or wild celery.

Though its uses were similar in the United States, some say that our variety is inferior to its European counterpart and not as aromatic. No matter. The stories surrounding it came with the species found in North America anyway.

Angelica was a plant long revered for its medical and folklore uses. It was said to ward off witches and evil spirits, perhaps a reference to its genus name. It was, after all, known as *"the Root of the Holy Ghost."* There's even mention of its use for exorcism by burning the dried leaves during rites to banish away the evil.

Another legend says that an angel disclosed that angelica was a cure for the plague. The plague peaked in Europe between 1348 and 1350, so you get an idea how long the stories have persisted. In fact, its use dates back even further to the 10th century. And if that wasn't enough, it was also said to protect you against rabid animals. It's perhaps a good thing then that the plant was and is so common.

Angelica crossed into many cultures. Hoodoo practitioners used its root for several purposes, including rites for breaking a jinx or turning your luck around, especially when it came to health issues.

Health issues, of course, include the heart, both figuratively and literally. Herbalists used angelica to ensure fidelity in a marriage. Curiously, there is also mention of its use as a poison, but whether that refers to its fidelity usage remains unclear. Suffice to say, it had both plan A and plan B uses.

Its poisonous reputation may be due to the acrid nature of its root that dissipates once the plant is dried, a quality you'll find in several plants in this volume. Both the seeds and roots pack the greatest punch. Nevertheless, angelica was and perhaps is, a fitting addition to the "*witch's garden*." That tidbit gives rise to its other stories.

Angelica has a mystical side too. It shared an association with the Sun, which may explain some of its reputed uses and healing properties. To realize its greatest power, you should plant it on a Sunday when the moon is waxing with other plants that have a similar relationship with the Sun, such as rosemary or St. John's wort.

More than the Sun favored sweet angelica however. It was said to be sacred to the goddess, Venus. It was also a plant traditionally associated with the Pagan Sabbath, Beltane on May 1st.

Historically, Beltane marked an important day in the Gaelic world. Summer begins. The cattle go to pasture. In preparation for the season ahead, the Sabbath bestowed blessings on the people and livestock so that all may go well. It was a happy time with rituals of all sorts.

It seems appropriate then that a plant believed to protect against evil should be a part of the festivities. Angelica remained important for both Christians and Pagans in this context as well as other popular uses into modern times.

Its use with magic and evils spirits was not limited to Europeans and the settlers. The Iroquois used it for similar purposes. One account mentions its use as a witchcraft medicine for punishing evil persons.

The literature doesn't mention what the punishment was, but it would undoubtedly be related to the unpleasantness associated with its root. Another use was for a wash to remove ghosts from one's home, perhaps similarly affected.

From an eating perspective, the leaf and root are edible when cooked. You can eat the stem like asparagus or add it to a salad. The stems also make a tasty celery substitute, hence, its other name of wild celery. You can even make a candy from the root by simmering it in some simple syrup. It does have some nutritional value as a source of vitamin B12, magnesium, and potassium.

In Europe, it is cultivated and used in the preparation of some alcoholic beverages, including gin, vermouth, Galliano, Drambuie, and Chartreuse to capture its unique flavor. This latter use is ironic given it history as a cure for alcoholism as well.

Ecology: Attracts butterflies

Medicinal Use

Its genus name, *Angelica,* is Latin for angelic, perhaps a reference to its medicinal properties. As far as a wild plant goes, it is quite striking when you stumble upon it. It almost appears tropical with its tall profile and reddish stalks.

Many stories exist about its purported cures that may offer clues about its chemistry. One story claimed it was a cure for typhoid. Europeans settlers, on the other hand, used angelica as an agent to make one perspire and as an emetic. It was also used for upper respiratory issues and as a gargle for sore throats. These early uses speak to its value in the herbalist toolkit. American Indians also used this native plant in similar ways.

The Menominee used angelica along with Canada wormwood as a poultice to relieve pain. By placing it on the opposite side of the body, it was said to draw the aches to the surface and away from the sufferer.

They also used this combination to treat suppressed menstruation, a treatment that the Cherokee used as well. The Cherokee used angelica for other purposes along these lines, including as a cold remedy and a tonic for "*nervous females.*" Given the cautions for ingesting this plant, some truth may exist with these claims.

Like the Cherokee, the Iroquois used angelica to treat a variety of respiratory conditions, such as pneumonia. They also applied it to broken bones and parts of the body affected by frostbite or exposure. Historically, it was used by several nations for treating headaches as well as for rheumatism when used in a steam bath.

Like many plants, herbalists used angelica as a blood purifier. Back in the day, healers might attribute health conditions to something wrong with the blood. You'll find frequents mentions of blood tonics, purifiers, and what-not in the literature. Perhaps this is one clue about where the term, "bad blood" comes from.

The chemical properties of angelica offers some clues about its supposed cures. One explanation may lie with its antimicrobial activity. Its carminative or gas-relieving properties could explain its use as a stimulating tonic or as a cure for digestive ailment, and hence, another of its common names, bellyache root.

There seems no end to its uses in the folklore, with other accounts in the literature speaking of its ability to improve energy and stimulate circulation. If you had to have one wild plant, you couldn't go wrong with some angelica in your satchel.

4 ASTER

Common name: Aster

Other names: White heath aster, Christmas daisy, starwort, Michaelmas daisy

Scientific name: *Aster pilosus*, Aster Family

Habitat: Dry prairies and meadows, disturbed sites

Season: Summer, fall

Status: Native

Type: Perennial forb

Identifying characteristics: Small, daisy-like white flowers with yellow center with hairy stems. Plant height is one to five feet tall.

Special cautions: If you have skin allergies, aster and many others of its kind pose some risks. Handling it may cause contact dermatitis in some individuals. In other words, the itching may drive you nuts if you're allergic to other plants in this family, like ragweed.

Folklore

I specify a particular species of aster. However, specific identification may give you trouble, with about 180 species in this genus. Many of the stories apply to white asters in general. Other than color, you may find the subtler differences hard to detect.

In any case, this delicate little flower has so many myths and legends associated with it that it may be hard to find a culture that has no association with it.

Some stories go back to the ancient Greeks and mythology. Other cultures also found uses for the aster. Pagans used it with the Sabbath, Autumn Equinox. This timing is fitting, given the fact that it flowers later in the season.

Asters were considered sacred to all gods and goddesses, especially Venus. It certainly had a romantic side. One myth states that asters were the tears of the goddess, Astraea, who wept when the last two humans wandered the land lost and alone after Zeus flooded the Earth as punishment for their evil ways. The story—and the name—stuck.

The ancients believed that asters possessed mystical powers, being able to ward off evil spirits and snakes. The Germans would burn them for this reason. The ancient world must have been a scary place with all of these plants for protection and evil doers. But herbalists didn't just use aster to guard against the dark forces.

Considered a talisman of love, a boiled mixture of aster leaves in wine could improve the quality of honey when placed near a beehive, wrote Virgil. Even if it didn't improve the honey, it could improve your mood and chances for love.

The other names for the aster refer to the flower and its life cycle. The name, starwort, literally means star flower. A fitting name, don't you think? The mention of Christmas and Michaelmas is a reference to its late blooming period, and perhaps the reason it is the flower of September.

Asters are one of the latest wildflowers to bloom in the summer. The species name, *pilosus*, means soft or hairy, referring to its hairy stem. This characteristic can help with identification.

Food: While other asters were used by American Indians, there are no indications that the white heath aster was eaten by them.

Ecology: It can be weedy and invasive. Despite this negative quality, it is of special value to bees and butterflies.

Medicinal Use

Some American Indians used aster medicinally in sweat lodges. Plants were placed on hot rocks to release a healing herbal steam. It was also said to be able to revive a person who was unconscious. While not used extensively, it does have scientifically verified anti-bacterial properties, so there may be some truth behind the stories.

5 BLOODROOT

Common name: Bloodroot

Other names: Red puccoon, paucon, Indian paint

Scientific name: *Sanguinaria canadensis*, Poppy Family

Habitat: Dry to moderately dry forests; usually in rich soil

Season: Spring

Status: Native

Type: Perennial forb

Identifying characteristics: Unusual paw-like leaves. The leaves are so distinctive that you can easily identify bloodroot no matter what the season if present.

It has showy daisy-like white flowers with a yellow disk flower. Plant height is under one foot tall. They often grow in carpets, making the flower a stunning addition to the landscape.

Special cautions: Bloodroot, as the name may imply, carries some risk. It contains opium-like alkaloids and may cause mucous membrane irritation. You can't collect bloodroot everywhere. It is protected in Rhode Island and New York.

Folklore

Its genus name, *Sanguinarius*, means bleeding in Latin, a reference to its red-colored sap. In the Midwest, it is one of the first spring wildflowers to bloom. Because of its preference for rich soils, its presence generally indicates an area of better ecological health. In any case, its beautiful white flowers are a welcome sight.

As you can imagine, bloodroot with its red sap had many uses. European settlers used it as a strong dye. American Indians used it as a face paint for this reason as well. They also used it to dye mats, baskets, and weapons.

While the flowers are short-lived, the sap runs in the plant for the entire season. If you snap a stem, you can see for yourself how vibrant—and potent—of a dye it is.

Perhaps because of the association of blood and the heart, bloodroot has a romantic side as well. The Algonquin used bloodroot as a love charm. Not to be outdone, the Micmac found a similar use for it as an aphrodisiac. If you wanted to marry your beloved, you should rub the plant on the palm of your hand and shake her hand, as the Ponca believed.

The Iroquois, on the other hand, had different ideas about what to do with bloodroot that ran contrary to these more romantic notions. They used bloodroot for treating "*women that are ugly.*" Your guess is as good as mine about what "*ugly*" may mean in this case. The literature does not expound on this particular use nor its efficacy.

Aside from ugly women, bloodroot served other purposes. If evil spirits were the problem, bloodroot could help. Planting it with other plants of protection such as angelica, lavender, or rosemary could help ward off any matter of evil spirits or misfortune. Potent stuff, to be sure! However, it was best to start your garden on a Sunday to better favor the gods.

The association with blood made for some darker uses of bloodroot as well you might expect. The Iroquois used it as a witchcraft medicine for use as a wash for a person who had seen a dead person. Apparently, its magic could extend to the undead.

Food: Not recommended as an edible plant. Read on to learn why.

Ecology: Sensitive to weather

Medicinal Use

American Indians used bloodroot extensively for medicinal purposes. The Ojibwa and Potawatomi used its juice with a bit of maple sugar as a cure for a sore throat. Bloodroot does have antibacterial and anti-inflammatory properties that support these uses. Many other nations used it for treating respiratory conditions too, such as the Cherokee and Iroquois, who even used it for treating hiccups.

The association with blood accounts for other uses that fall under the category of blood and circulation. The Algonquin believed chewing the root could treat heart trouble, a use shared by the Delaware, Iroquois, and Ontario peoples. It could be used to treat bleeding or as in the case of the Penobscot, to prevent it. You win either way!

There are several accounts of using bloodroot to treat digestive ills, including stomach cramps, ulcers, and indigestion. If you had tapeworms, a bit of bloodroot with some whiskey would do the job, or so said the Iroquois. But, then again, whiskey has medicinal properties of its own too. I'll leave that claim up to you, dear Reader.

As with many plants, bloodroot found its way into aspects of everyday life. Herbalists believed it was a blood purifier for treating colds and frazzled nerves. Its expectorant properties may explain the infusion with liquor that the Iroquois used as a cough medicine. It's interesting to note this infusion in particular if you consider the ingredients in over-the-counter medicines. A good night's sleep, after all, is a great healer.

As with all good plants, bloodroot uses didn't stop there. If you needed to build up your strength, a bit of root taken every morning for a month would cure you, as the Delaware believed. The literature doesn't explain why you must take it for a month.

Considering its other medicinal properties, it could have taken the edge off of anything that could be sapping your strength. Herbalists also used it for treating fits or as a general panacea to add to its toolbox qualities.

The folklore contains references to using the root powder for childbirth and as a root tea for muscle pain and menstrual cramps. Pain relief was a reoccurring theme with bloodroot. Herbalists prescribed chewing the root to treat burns and infections too.

It was used to remove slivers and thorns as well as a first aid for treating sores and wounds. And its use was not limited to humans. Bloodroot was also a veterinary aid for inducing abortion in horses by the Abnaki of northeastern North America. That particular usage may raise some eyebrows about humans ingesting it.

Stranger things have happened. Because of its antimicrobial and plaque-fighting properties, bloodroot extract was an ingredient in toothpastes and mouthwashes into the modern age. However, it has since disappeared from use in recent years. It started out well before matters took a turn, as you may expect.

In the 1800s, doctors used a salve made from bloodroot to treat skin growths. Later scientific research has confirmed its immune-stimulating effects.

However, the literature also contains several accounts of this ointment causing lesions rather than treating them. Some reports from the 1800s mention deaths caused by ingesting a bloodroot tincture. It is best to stick to enjoying the stories and beauty of bloodroot rather than its would-be medicinal uses.

6 BUTTER AND EGGS

Common name: Butter and Eggs

Other names: Wild snapdragon, toadflax, flaxweed, ramsted, Jacob's ladder

Scientific name: *Linaria vulgaris*, Figwort Family

Habitat: Disturbed sites

Season: Summer, fall

Status: Introduced

Type: Perennial forb

Identifying characteristics: Spike with yellow to orange flowers that have a lighter exterior and a deeper colored lip. Plant height is one to three feet tall

Special cautions: Butter and eggs has a strong odor, which may get on your hands if you collect it or plants near it. Like many wild plants, pregnant women should avoid using it.

In any case, caution is a good plan for anyone using this plant. It carries a risk of being toxic in incorrect dosages. In addition, butter and eggs is considered a noxious weed in several states, including Idaho, Montana,

Nevada, New Mexico, Oregon, South Dakota, Washington, and Wyoming. This means you can collect it, but may not sell or grow it. Additional restrictions may apply.

Folklore

The story goes that this plant was brought to America by a Welsh man named Ramsted, hence, one of its common names, ramsted. Butter and eggs had a wide array of uses, which vary with the culture.

Historically, it was used as plant dye with a lovely yellow hue. It had other uses in the home, including as a fly poison when boiled in milk and curiously, also for skin lotions. The concurrent uses probably helped if you were plagued by flies.

The Scots had their own uses for butter and eggs. It was said that if you walk around the plant three times, it would break any spell that may have been cast on you. These are the kinds of stories I'd love to hear about the precise origins. Three times? Was whisky involved?

Not to be outdone, the English also viewed it similarly, saying that putting three seeds on a linen thread would guard against evil. Three appears to be the key when dealing with butter and eggs.

Ecology: The plant can be weedy and invasive, which explains its classification as a noxious weed in some areas. Resistance to pesticides has also been reported, which makes sense given that it was used as an insecticide. Because of its status, be careful about possible pesticide contact.

Medicinal Use

A tea made from butter and eggs was a folk cure for a diverse range of ailments, including constipation, conjunctivitis, and jaundice. It acts primarily on the liver, which can explain many of its early uses. One has to wonder though about three so diverse uses.

Butter and eggs has a lot going for it, having anti-inflammatory, diuretic, and purgative properties. But it also spells caution when using it because it can have an effect on such an important organ like the liver. This is sage advice, indeed, for any plant that can act on any vital organ.

Butter and eggs has its own Doctrine of Signatures. Because its flowers resembled a person saying "Ah," the folklore believed it was a cure for throat ailments. To others, it resembles more of a toad, hence, the name, toadflax. Either one makes sense, I suppose.

It was believed to be an effective treatment for all sorts of skin maladies. It could treat something as simple as redness and inflammation to hemorrhoids to more serious conditions such as skin ulcers. The literature even includes references to its use for deformities, such as leprosy.

The Ojibwa used toadflax in combination with other foliage as an inhalant in medicine lodges, going back to its own Doctrine of Signatures. The literature also makes reference to its use for sores and skin conditions.

The Iroquois valued it for its use for digestive complaints and as an emetic. Like many wild plants, the folklore held a bit of truth. Medical research has confirmed its antioxidant properties.

Butter and eggs has other types of associations with American Indians. Making use of its sedative properties, the Iroquois gave to crying babies. They would also use it to remove bewitching, perhaps causing the babies to cry in the first place.

The Iroquois had other curious uses. An infusion of the plants could induce vomiting, a good thing when it's necessary. However, this use was as an anti-love medicine. Despite its attractive appearance, this plant has not fared well through the ages. Too bad for a plant with such a whimsical name.

7 CATNIP

Common name: Catnip

Other names: Catsmint, catwort, field balm

Scientific name: *Nepeta cataria*, Mint Family

Habitat: Dry woods, disturbed sites

Season: Summer, fall

Status: Introduced

Type: Perennial forb

Identifying characteristics: Cream to light lavender flowers, with darker spots. Leaves opposite and textured. It is highly aromatic. In fact, you may likely smell the plant before you see it. Its height is about one to three feet tall.

Special cautions: Pregnant women should avoid ingesting catnip, but that goes without saying.

Folklore

Wild catnip is the same thing as the kind you buy at the store for your cat, with the all the same effects. You may find it is more potent and your cat more lively though with the wild type, if just because it's fresher. You can gather the flowers and dry them for a treat for your pet, though the leaves work just as well. Be sure and wash your hands afterward though; its strong and some would say disagreeable scent, tends to linger.

The species name, *cataria*, comes from the Latin meaning cat, appropriately enough. It has a very different effect on people though than in cats. With people, it acts more like a sedative and induces sleep rather than acting as stimulant and making you chase imaginary mice as it does in cats.

This explains its use as a folk cure for restlessness in children or colic in babies. A bit of warm catnip tea could do the trick. However, cats will snooze too if they eat the leaves and flowers rather than just roll in them.

The old ones believed catnip could ward off nightmares and the evil eye, all of which contributes to a good night's sleep. Another legend says that catnip was one of several herbs used to conjure spirits and cat magic, perhaps to accomplish these same purposes.

There's no doubt that the ancients believed something mystical existed with catnip. Some used an incense made from the dried plant to consecrate magical tools. It was also said to be sacred to Bast, the ancient Egyptian goddess of sensual pleasure. Its bewitching qualities apparently had no bound. Maybe that's why cats like it so well.

Like many aromatic plants, catnip has insect-repellent properties, a good reason to let a stand keep growing in your yard. Catnip contains a chemical called nepetalactone that research has shown to be effective against mosquitoes. It has even proven more effective and safer than the commercial chemical, DEET for this task. But note that this effect is for mosquitoes and not ticks. You still need the heavy artillery for them.

Some accounts include fleas and ants too as victims of this particular charm. But, wait, there's more. The folklore mentions that it also repels rats. In some areas it was grown as protection against them. Along with repelling the evil spirits, you could rest assured that your home was safe with catnip.

Food: The dried leaves make a pleasant-tasting tea. In France, it is cultivated as a seasoning.

Ecology: Catnips attracts honeybees, lots of honeybees. Catnip can be weedy and invasive like most plants in the Mint family. If you want to grow it at home, you might consider keeping it in a pot rather than in the garden to keep it under control, though it will likely escape into your garden anyway.

Medicinal Use

Herbalists used catnip primarily for respiratory conditions. A tea made from the leaves was said to treat colds, bronchitis, and chicken pox. The Menominee even used for it for treating pneumonia.

If you had a fever, a poultice placed on your forehead could provide relief, according to the Iroquois. The plant is high in vitamins C and E, which can explain these uses and some of the seemingly miraculous qualities it possesses.

Herbalists used catnip for other medicinal purposes, including as a substance to induce menstruation, which is why pregnant women should avoid it. Nevertheless, catnip had a strong historical association with motherhood and childbirth. It was said that catnip could treat barrenness and the pains of labor.

It found uses in other applications outside of the birthing area. Herbalists used catnip to treat a variety of digestive issues in children and adults, in addition to its soporific properties. It could relieve any matter of stomach or abdominal cramps or aches from colds.

Part of its efficacy came from the other effects it could bring about. For example, it could stimulate sweating, which would in turn, could reduce fevers. In addition, chewing the leaves was said to cure a toothache. The Ojibwa even used it as a blood purifier.

Both the Menominee and Ojibwa used catnip to allay hysteria, undoubtedly due to its calming properties. A good nap, after all, could cure most ills.

The Cherokee also used it to treat spasms. Because of its sedative properties, it was used a "*children tonic*" by some, such as the Delaware, Rappahannock, and Iroquois peoples. After all, sometimes, the best child is the one who sleeps.

Other documented uses include other parts of the plant, including the use of a leaf tea for colds, digestion, fever, and respiratory conditions. A leaf poultice was said to be just the thing for treating inflammation and swelling. This latter use is validated by research that demonstrates its antioxidant activity.

8 CATTAIL

Common name: Cattail

Other names: Broadleaf cattail, common cattail, catnine tail, punks, cat-o-nine tails

Scientific name: *Typha latifolia*, Cattail Family

Habitat: Wetlands, marshes, shallows

Season: Spring, summer

Status: Native

Type: Perennial forb

Identifying characteristics: Long blades, usually found in clumps or dense stands. Brown elongated seed head. Plant height is three to nine feet tall.

Special cautions: Wetlands that contain cattails may also have threatened or endangered plants in the area. These sites may be nesting habitat for birds and other wildlife. Be careful of them when collecting—as aggressive water snakes like these habitats too! Like all plants, be sure of your identification. Cattails may share the habitat with the poisonous iris, poisonous hemlock, and stinging nettles.

And as if that weren't enough, a modern-day risk exists with cattails as well. Pollutants and contaminants can accumulate in cattails plants. Stick to collecting it in clean waters to minimize your risks.

Folklore

You'll likely find cattails dominating wetland habitats. North America has two species, common and narrow-leaved cattail. Either variety will do, depending upon where you are. It's found in virtually any place that is wet. You won't have any problems finding it.

Ecologists refer to this plant as a colonizer because it'll take advantage of any bit of open muddy soil to establish itself. They can be quite aggressive and difficult to remove once established. Finding a good use for them, therefore, made sense back in the day.

Cattail has a rich history of use simply because virtually the entire plant is edible and useful. With the American Indians, there are 71 different documented uses alone. The young shoots or corms can be cooked like potatoes. You can eat the flower heads, which once boiled, are not unlike corn on the cob.

You can also can make flour from the pollen, albeit an arduous task at best. Imagine walking through a dense wetlands, tapping the cattails over a paper bag to collect the powder-like pollen for flour. It would definitely be a labor of love, I'd say.

Cattails had more practical uses too, such as using the seed fuzz for makeshift diapers or feminine hygiene products. You could also use it as down for pillows and blankets, as well as insulation to tuck into your boots to prevent frostbite. Its leaves were woven into mats, baskets, and bedding that was dense for good insulation.

Cattail also had ceremonial significance. There are numerous uses in the record. The Navajo, for example, used it as a ceremonial emetic, while the Ojibwa used it as war medicine. The Keres shook the ripened cattails in rain dance ceremonies. The Apache used the pollen in many ceremonies and rituals. With its inflammable pollen, it could easily serve as fuel or tinder or even rush lights when needed.

The folklore had a different take on the Doctrine of Signatures associated with the cattail than the typical medicinal or mystical use. There is mention of its association with lust, perhaps because of the phallic shape of its seed head.

Ecology: Muskrats eat and build with cattails. Waterfowl may, in turn, use the muskrat lodges for nesting platforms, which leads to another caution. A goose on the nest or with young goslings is a formidable adversary. Don't even try. Back away from the muskrat lodge, slowly.

Medicinal Use

Cattails were used medicinally by settlers and American Indians as well with this most useful plant. It was given to both animals and women in labor to prevent hemorrhaging and for treating bleeding wounds in horses. Its anticoagulant and suppurative properties undoubtedly helped.

As far as other people applications, the Iroquois used an infusion as a wash for bleeding sores. There are even accounts of its use for a bleeding navel in infants by the Mahuna people. Who would have thought?

American Indians had scores of other uses for cattails. A poultice made from the roots treated wounds and burns and was used by many nations, including the Algonquin and Cahuilla. The Dakota and Montana peoples used it for a dressing for burns probably because it made a good poultice that would hold up.

Truth supports the history. Science has confirmed that cattail has wound-healing properties, which may have served people well for these uses.

In addition to being a staple food and general healer, cattails helped treat other conditions, such as abdominal cramps and kidney stones. The Houma people even used it for treating whooping cough.

And you didn't have to eat it to get the benefits. The Iroquois believed that cysts on the breast could be cured by sleeping on a mat made from cattails. Kind of makes you want to start a stand of cattails in your yard now, doesn't it?

9 CHICKWEED

Common name: Chickweed

Other names: Common chickweed

Scientific name: *Stellaria media*, Pink Family

Habitat: Disturbed areas, meadows

Season: Spring through fall

Status: Introduced

Type: Annual/perennial forb

Identifying characteristics: Daisy-like flower with opposite leaves. Height less than 16 inches tall. You'll likely find it in your lawn, at the park, or in other green spaces.

Special cautions: Large quantities of chickweed may have a laxative effect. It also contains high amounts of nitrates, which can cause methemoglobinemia, or "*blue baby*" disease. There's a good reason why the USDA has a zero-tolerance for added nitrate in food destined for infants and children under 2.

Folklore

The demure chickweed is endearing because of its trait of "sleeping" at night, when the leaves fold over the buds. It is an abundant plant that is very easy to find, if just in your lawn. In fact, it is the most common weed in the world, found even in north Arctic regions.

Several old wives tales exist about chickweed, to be expected with a plant so common. One tale claims that if the flowers are open by 10 a.m., it will not rain that day. Another story says that if you see the flowers closed, it will rain within four hours. The Weather Channel has nothing on the sweet little chickweed!

For being such a little and demure plant, chickweed is quite hardy. It colonizes disturbed ground, which may not be the healthiest habitats around. It can tolerate cold surprisingly well.

Food: Leaves can be added to salads or dried for a pleasant tea. You can also boil them and serve as a green. Chickweed is highly nutritious and a good source of calcium and magnesium.

However, chickweed contains saponins, which give it soap-like foaming activity. It may cause gastrointestinal distress at high doses. Best to enjoy it in moderation.

Ecology: Food plant for birds and rabbits

Medicinal Use

Chickweed has numerous medicinal qualities that factor into its folklore use. You'd be hard pressed to find some ailment that it wasn't used to treat. It has diuretic and expectorant properties. The latter explains its use for treating coughs and colds. A decoction made from the entire plant served as a heart tonic and was also given to women after childbirth.

Like many wild plants, chickweed was used to treat liver ailments. It was said you could find relief by applying the juice of the bruised plant to the area of your liver with a cloth soaked in it.

Chickweed also had topical uses, including some surprising ones. The literature reports that a leaf concoction was used as an eye wash. Other uses include digestive and kidney ailments as well as dermatitis and itchy skin.

It was said to speed healing and soothe skin irritations. A warm poultice could do wonders for you. An old husband's tale says that it was even a cure for obesity. But where it goes from itchy skin to losing weight is anyone's guess.

The American Indians did not use it extensively. There are accounts that the Chippewa used a leaf decoction as an eye wash as well. Other accounts speak of using the expressed juice for the same purpose.

The Iroquois also used it for treating swelling, cuts and wounds. This use makes sense, given its astringent and soothing properties. Given these traits and being an anti-inflammatory could also explain its effectiveness for treating rheumatic pain. It is yet another example of how a grain of truth exists in some of these old stories.

Research has shown that chickweed has antimicrobial activity. Some studies have found that compounds isolated from chickweed seeds may provide a means for controlling fungal diseases in other plants. Other uses have not been confirmed, though it hasn't stopped people finding more ways to use chickweed.

10 CHICORY

Common name: Chicory

Other names: French endive, succory, blue sailors, coffeeweed, ragged sailors, blue dandelion, blue daisy

Scientific name: *Cichorium intybus*, Aster Family

Habitat: Disturbed areas, roadsides

Season: Summer

Status: Introduced

Type: Perennial forb

Identifying characteristics: Lavender daisy-like flowers with no center disk. Flowers go down the stem, making the plant appear sparse. Plant height is about one to six feet tall.

Edible parts: Leaves, root

Special cautions: It is considered a noxious weed in Colorado. Beware of plants that may have been sprayed with pesticide.

Folklore

The use of chicory goes back to the ancient Greeks, Romans, and Egyptians. Horace, the Roman poet, praised its virtues in 65 BC. The long history of use certainly must make for some good stories, of which chicory has plenty.

Roasted roots make a delicious coffee. Early Europeans mixed it with regular coffee in England and France back in the day. The young roots taste best, however, while the older ones—older than two years—tend to be bitter.

The same can be said of the leaves, which are likewise bitter when the plant is in bloom. It's best to blanch them before eating them to counteract the unpleasant taste. Then, it'll make a tasty addition to your salad. However, the root was also cooked and eaten like parsnips.

Settlers even grew it as a forage crop. It was a good choice indeed. The plant provides a good source of several nutrients, including potassium, calcium, and vitamins A and C.

You may think that this use is curious given the lowly state of chicory today where it is left to grow on littered roadsides. To think that one time it was a valued crop! Where's the love?

Speaking of love, chicory also had a use in affairs of the heart, which may stem from a German legend that gives chicory its other name, "*watcher of the road.*" You know the story; every culture has one.

Legend says that a young girl perished tragically of a broken heart when her lover failed to return from [you fill in the blank]. She was said to have died along a road, a site where you typically find this plant growing. The story may have given rise to its use for making love potions, specifically those for keeping your lover faithful.

Another legend says that chicory sprung from the unrequited love of the Sun. A maiden spurred him and was turned into the flower. For punishment, she had to gaze upon the Sun and remember her transgression for all time.

Indeed, the flower opens in the morning and closes at noon, when the Sun is strongest overhead. Chicory is truly a plant of summer, flowering from the middle to close to the end of the season. When you see it appear, you know that fall is soon to come.

The folklore makes mention of several magical uses. It was said to be an important plant for removing obstacles in one's life. While the literature doesn't mention what type of obstacles, being secretive may be one of them.

There are stories speaking of its use for invisibility if gathered at the witching hour on Midsummer. Alas, there is no confirmation about this use either.

Medicinal Use

The folk uses for chicory were many. It was a tonic for fevers and jaundice because of its cooling properties. Some believed it could lower blood sugar.

The latter isn't a stretch because of its inulin content. Several plants contains this naturally-occurring polysaccharide, including wheat and garlic. In fact, food manufacturers use inulin in processed foods for flavoring. The FDA has classified it as generally recognized as safe (GRAS).

Chicory also has a slight sedative effect, not unlike catnip. This fact may explain the Cherokee's use as a root infusion as a tonic for nerves. Some research suggests that chicory may lower one's heart rate, which would also support this claim.

The old ones believed that it was the liver's friend. The writings of Homer and Pliny make mention of it. Herbalists used it for a variety of maladies from jaundice to gout to rheumatism. It was the cure that tasted good—literally. The plant contains a concentration of three sugars that account for its pleasant taste.

A leaf poultice was a general cure-all for treating inflammation and swelling. It was even used as an eye wash for treating inflamed eyes. Sore eyes must have been a common complaint back in the day, given the number of remedies used to treat it.

The Iroquois used it as well for as a poultice and wash for treating fever sores. Chicory also has diuretic properties that can help remove excess water in the body without depleting potassium stores. This property makes it similar to other potassium-sparing diuretics like amiloride or eplerenone. That trait may explain why it was used as a poultice and anti-inflammatory agent.

Research has confirmed some of its historical uses. One study suggested that chicory may be an effective means to control pathogens in livestock, especially when fed during stressful periods. For humans, chicory contains chemicals that can prevent cavities, the most common oral infectious disease in the world. Oh, the irony given its sugar content!

You will chicory among the Bach flower remedies developed by Edward Bach, an English homoeopath, in the 1930s. Rather than being a cure for the eternal conflict between the soul and actions, the homoeopathic remedies may act best as a placebo.

11 CINQUEFOIL

Common name: Cinquefoil

Other names: Five fingers, oldfield cinquefoil, goose grass, meadown nut, good tansy (not to be confused with the real tansy that is not edible, or at least shouldn't be)

Scientific name: *Potentilla simplex*, Rose Family

Habitat: Dry forests and meadows

Season: Spring, summer

Status: Native

Type: Perennial forb

Identifying characteristics: Small yellow flowers, with red stems and five-part toothed leaves. Plant height is under one foot tall.

Special cautions: n/a

Folklore

Cinquefoil's genus name, *Potentilla*, is derived from the Latin word "potens," meaning powerful. This tidbit gives you a clue about its uses and what herbalists thought about it. At a time when magic ruled the world, cinquefoil ranked high among plants used for mystical purposes.

It was an ingredient in a potent witch's brew consisting of other plants, such as nightshade and hemlock, both of which pack a punch in their own right. You might also find it in a potion used for inducing trances.

Some uses traversed a darker realm. The literature contains a gruesome tale of its use as a "witch's ointment," which is mixed with wolfsbane and the fat of dead children retrieved from their graves. While its purpose may be unclear, the folklore mentions cinquefoil as an ingredient in concoctions that made witches able to fly.

Despite these sinister uses, it was used to protect one from witches as well, especially when hung around doors and windows. The folklore provides several specific ways to use cinquefoil.

One legend says that you should gather cinquefoil and place in a red bag to hang over your bed. Then, at sunrise every Sunday, you should anoint it with a protection oil.

Another tale says that you can banish incubus or succubus demons by gathering it on the morning of the Summer Solstice in June. If you plant cinquefoil on a Sunday, you could also ward off evil spirits.

Many other stories exist about cinquefoil, presumably because of the witch association. Herbalists believed that a pregnant woman could determine the sex of her unborn child by drinking a tea made from its flowers. If the blooms were white, you would have a girl. If you wanted a boy, you should seek out the yellow ones.

Food: Leaves and shoots in salad or cooked as a vegetable

Ecology: Minor food value to birds and small mammals

Medicinal Use

The folklore is filled with uses of cinquefoil for various bacterial issues. Like many all-purpose cures, herbalists also used it to treat an individual with a sore throat or fever. Indeed, you might even receive a concoction with cinquefoil for loose teeth as well as "*spongy gums*." And a wash made with cinquefoil could soothe irritated skin and wounds presumably because of its antiseptic and astringent qualities.

I'd be remiss if I didn't mention the ubiquitous digestive and blood ailment uses. The American Indians used a root tea to treat a variety of digestive complaints. Some believed that cinquefoil could stop bleeding.

It even has anti-wrinkle properties. The Cherokee had several uses for it, including as mouthwash and as a tonic for fevers and dysentery. Research has shown that it has strong anti-fungal potential, which confirms some of its historical uses.

Some may mistake cinquefoil, also known as five-leaf grass, for other plants having a similar characteristic. Other than making witches fly, the literature is silent about any other unworldly effects or snack-craving tendencies.

12 COLUMBINE

Common name: Columbine

Other names: Red columbine, wild columbine, meeting-houses, honeysuckle

Scientific name: *Aquilegia canadensis*, Buttercup Family

Habitat: Dry forests, cliffs

Season: Spring, summer

Status: Native

Type: Perennial forb

Identifying characteristics: Red to deep red tubular flowers with yellow stamens that extend outside of the flower. Lobed three-part leaves. Plant height is one to three feet tall

Special cautions: Columbine is endangered in Florida, so keep your paws off!

Folklore

The name, columbine, comes from the Latin word, columba, meaning dove or pigeon. It is a reference to the flower's resemblance to a bird. Okay. And indeed, its genus name, *Aquilegia*, comes from the Latin for talons. This association with columbine and birds has persisted through the ages even back to the Saxons. They called it culverwort, meaning pigeon plant.

Author, Neltje Blanchan, describes columbine in a much more romantic fashion, referring to its elfin charm as ". . . it coquettes with some Punchinello." Its rich red color and delicate stature certainly could inspire such fancy.

Unfortunately, the folklore contains less enchanting tales too. Columbine has a varied and sometimes unfortunate history. It was said to be the symbol of a deserted lover, bad for either a woman or man. However, despite these stories, the coquettish columbine has other secrets to tell.

American Indians including the Omaha people used the crushed seeds as a love charm. The Ponca and Pawnee also used the seeds for this purpose. Rather than dismissing a lover, columbine attracted one. Bachelors, it was said, used columbine as a cologne in the affairs of the heart. Its scent is sweet and delicate, a fact not lost on hummingbirds. If you plant it, they will come.

There is mention of the flower being a food source, but caution is in order. The plant contains prussic acid or hydrocyanic acid and may have a narcotic effect. Grazing animals like cows and sheep, sometimes die from poisoning from feeding on plants like sorghum which also contains this same compound. Perhaps these accounts explain its sometimes less than perfect standing in the folklore.

However, its toxic quality may account for some of columbine's other uses because there's always another side to the story. The Iroquois, for example, used it as a witch medicine for detecting bewitchment.

This use is curious given the fact that the Meskwaki believed that a decoction of the plant could give one the power of persuasion at trade or in council. Perhaps these claims account for an old husband's tale that says that lions would eat columbine to build up their strength. That power of persuasion worked for columbine as well.

Food: Flowers only with caution. There is that prussic acid thing.

Ecology: Columbine has the unique ability of self-fertilization to produce seeds even when pollinators are absent.

Medicinal Use

Herbalists used columbine to treat liver conditions like jaundice, especially when taken with saffron in a little bit of wine. They also used it for treating sore throats and mouths. I'm not sure about the wine though in this concoctions, but it probably couldn't hurt.

Herbalists used it for other ailments, such as chicken pox and measles. The Iroquois used an infusion for treating poison ivy, which may explains why it was used for treating these conditions. One account even mentions that it was a cure for head lice. There must be some anti-histamine properties in it that made it work. But even if it wasn't effective, it would make a pleasant cure with its delightful, long-lingering scent.

Several American Indians nations used the columbine for treating a variety of digestive complaints. The Ojibwa believed it to be a powerful stomach tonic, while the Iroquois used it for treating kidney issues. There are also accounts of it being used for its analgesic qualities to treat headaches and fevers. Its astringent and anti-spasmodic properties might account for these uses.

The folklore makes mention of other uses such as a tea for the heart. Some settlers used it as a medicine to treat scurvy and smallpox. It wasn't a cure without risks though. Linnaeus talked of the plant being used in Europe for treating children, who unfortunately, were sometimes poisoned. There's that pesky prussic acid again.

13 CREEPING CHARLIE

Common name: Creeping Charlie

Other names: Ground ivy, gill-over-the-ground, haymaids, alehoof, Lizzy-run-up-the-Hedge, hedgemaids

Scientific name: *Glechoma hederacea*, Mint Family

Habitat: Disturbed sites, lawns

Season: Spring, summer

Status: Introduced

Type: Perennial forb

Identifying characteristics: Lavender to blue lipped flowers. Square stems, ivy like. It is aromatic when crushed or tread upon, which inspired some of its historic uses before becoming a tenacious weed. Plant height is under two feet.

Special cautions: It is considered a noxious weed in Connecticut perhaps with good reason. It is toxic to horses, especially when eaten in large quantities. Other livestock avoids it as well, including cattle and goats.

Folklore

Despite its infamous reputation in lawn care circles, ground ivy was once a revered plant, believe it or not. Its use goes back to the Saxons who used it to clarify their beer. Its aromatic nature undoubtedly added a distinctive taste too, which was later replaced by hops.

These uses explain the origin of some of its other names, such as the rather curious name, alehoof. Today, it is planted as a ground cover in England, a fact that may shock some American gardeners. In America, creeping Charlie makes its way into lawns just fine on its own.

Lest we do be too hasty to get rid of it, it bears mentioning that creeping Charlie also had magical associations. It was said to be a plant used for divination. The literature remains silent on whether that use had anything to do with the beer-making. In any case, it has some edible value.

Its leaves have a pleasant taste when added to salads. It also was dried for use as a tea. It was enjoyed as a cooling beverage known as Gill Tea back in the day. All you need to brew up a batch was some ground ivy, hot water, and a wee bit of honey to sweeten the concoction.

Medicinal Use

Ground ivy has a long history of medicinal use. Early herbalists considered it a spring tonic, presumably because of its high concentrations of vitamin C. It was also used to treat colds and allergies, which again might again be related to its nutritional value.

It has anti-histaminic and antibacterial properties that may further support using it for colds and sneezing. And that's not all. If you had a headache that wouldn't go away, the juice of ground ivy would do the trick.

During a time when the causes of medical conditions were unknown, plants like ground ivy had almost supernatural-like qualities. A vitamin C deficiency responds well to supplementation. And if it worked for some ailments, it certainly had to work for others.

Herbalist used ground ivy as a tonic for the digestive system and as an eye wash. Like many wild plants, it was used as a poultice for treating wounds and bruises. It was even touted as a cure for consumption. All of these uses relate back to its anti-microbial activity, so it may have done some good, if just for the placebo effect.

There are few accounts of American Indians using ground ivy. The Cherokee used an infusion for treating colds like many others who used it similarly. They also used it for hives and measles and hopefully, provided the sufferer with some relief. Other historical uses include a treatment for kidney ailments. It was said to cure backaches when boiled in mutton broth.

The evidence supporting the use of ground ivy may have you reconsidering your opinion of this common weed. Research has confirmed its antioxidant and anti-inflammatory properties.

Ironically enough, it has been shown to be an effective biological control of certain pests. If it wasn't ground ivy in your lawn, it might be some other weed. Pick your poison as the case may be.

Finally, ground ivy may inhibit the formation of tumors. These findings may confirm its use as a folklore cancer remedy. As with many wild plants, some uses have a kernel of truth in them. That's something to think about when you pull out the post-emergent broadleaf weed killer.

14 DANDELION

Common name: Dandelion

Other names: Faceclock, common dandelion, blowball, swine's snout

Scientific name: *Taraxacum officinale*, Aster Family

Habitat: Disturbed sites, lawns and my backyard

Season: Spring, summer

Status: Native and introduced

Type: Perennial forb

Identifying characteristics: Yellow dense flower with basal leaves. Plant height is less than one foot tall. But everyone knows what dandelions look like. Goat's beard is a larger, similar-looking species.

Edible parts: leaf, flower, root

Special cautions: Do not consume dandelion if you have diabetes or take an anticoagulant or diuretic. Its own diuretic properties may interfere with your medication. Some individuals may experience contact dermatitis from handling the plant because of the sap.

Folklore

Perhaps no wild plant says weed more than the lowly dandelion. Despite that, dandelion ranks as one of the most versatile and nutritious of all the ones discussed in this volume. Get ready to be amazed.

If you spend time removing them from your lawn, you may be surprised to learn that at one time English settlers imported and planted dandelions here across the pond. It was *that* valuable and tasty. Today, it is found in all 50 states and Canada. And there are several good reasons for this.

The dandelion was reputed to have magical properties, which may make you think differently about it. One could use it to develop one's psychic abilities for foretelling the future. You could also use it to call in the spirits, which may have helped your abilities.

It was even believed to be an indicator of weather. Before a storm, it is said that the flowers will close, not unlike chickweed. Nature offers many clues about weather if you take the time to look. Dandelion and chickweed are proof of that adage.

If you wanted to take advantage of its mystical properties, you should plant it in a garden with other plants that possess similar qualities, such as sweet grass. Sweet grass could invite good things, so it makes sense if you're using it this way. You could increase its effectiveness by adding a bit of dirt from a graveyard, which you naturally gathered on a full moon.

In addition to the European uses, the American Indians used it in similar ways. The Iroquois used it both as a love medicine and a tonic against witches. The connection with witches wasn't isolated. It was said to be sacred to Hecate, the Greek goddess of magic and witchcraft.

On the domestic front, the bright yellow flowers make an attractive plant dye. They can also be used as the basis for a pleasant-tasting dandelion wine or a dandelion beer.

Having tried a homemade version of the wine, I can personally vouch for its delightful taste. The making of the wine is a common practice. I remember talking with a local wine purveyor who told me that he would pay school kids to collect the yellow flowers in the spring for the batches he'd later brew. Just add some honey, cloves, lemon and lime slices, and you have quite the beverage.

In addition to its quaffable qualities, dandelion also deserves some props for its nutritional value. The leaves make a good source of calcium, vitamins A and C as well as magnesium and potassium. In fact, a 100 g serving will provide almost 10 percent of an adult's RDA for the latter. It is also an important source of lecithin, a compound that may help boost memory. If that isn't a reason to sample some dandelion wine, I don't know what is.

If wine isn't your thing, the roasted roots make a good coffee substitute. They don't contain caffeine, yet is said to have a stimulant effect. I made the coffee once. Other than being a bit of work to gather the roots, it made a decent cuppa.

Dandelion also makes good food stuffs. Several American Indian nations consumed dandelions as part of their diet, including the Ojibwa and Potawatomi who prepared it with a maple sap vinegar to serve with venison. Now, doesn't that sound tasty?

Today, both roots and leaves are used as flavorings in herbal beverages and as a dietary supplement. I was surprised to see dandelion among the high-priced specialty teas at my grocery store the other day. I guess everything comes full circle.

Ecology: Minor food value to birds

Medicinal Use

The dandelion holds a special, albeit, negative, significance for me. If I hadn't decided to make dandelion coffee, I might never have contracted the worst case of poison ivy that I ever have had to date.

The roots of the plant are a lot smaller, figuratively speaking, when you have to dig them up for something tasty like coffee than when you're weeding your garden. It took me quite a while to gather enough to make a decent-sized batch for roasting. A lot of digging meant a lot of contact time with poison ivy, definitely, a lesson in checking out a site before collecting.

Dandelion has several medicinal properties that explains its extensive use for things other than coffee and wine. It has strong antibacterial qualities against several bacteria strains including *Streptococcus pneumoniae*, or *pneumococcus* and *Staphylococcus aureus*. This makes for good information when faced with contact dermatitis.

It was like aspirin in the medicine cabinet for herbalists. It served many functions for many people as a tonic for treating a variety of complaints from jaundice to dermatitis to high blood pressure.

The latter is probably due to its diuretic properties. A diuretic is among the many choices available today for treating hypertension. Which leads to this caution. If you take a diuretic, you should avoid taking herbal supplements with dandelion to prevent overdosing—including dandelion found in the wild.

In any case, you can call the dandelion, the Swiss knife of medicinal plants. Herbalists used the entire plant, including the sap to remove warts. You should use caution, however, with this particular use. Some individuals may react to the plant's latex.

Adding to its laundry list of uses, dandelion was said to reduce cholesterol and to even help one lose weight. As with treating high blood pressure, its diuretic properties may have given rise to these latter claims. The fact that the leaves have laxative properties provides further fodder for its use as well.

And like many medicinal and edible plants, dandelion has a long history in the herbalist realm. The use of dandelion dates back to the tenth century when Arabian physicians used dandelion or wild endive, as they called it.

Today, it is a common dietary supplement. The German Commission E, a scientific advisory not unlike the FDA, have approved it for some uses, including appetite loss and urinary tract infections. Some of its folklore uses has a bit of truth to them.

But like most plants, dandelion also has its share of peculiar stories. One legend says that if you eat a dandelion salad on Mondays and Thursdays, you will stay healthy. The folklore gives us no reason why these days in particular should be beneficial.

Another story says that if you want to keep rheumatism at bay, you should drink a cup of dandelion tea every day in the morning and in the evening. But dandelion's miraculous powers don't end here.

Another folklore legend says that it will cure night blindness. The fact that it is high in vitamins A and C may explain its health value for these uses. It might have helped a wee bit.

The Menominee ate the greens, but did not use it medicinally. Other American Indian nations used it for several other health issues. The Ojibwa, for example, made a tea from the root for treating heartburn. Several others used dandelion for various digestive issues. It was also used as that universal blood tonic by other peoples, including the Iroquois.

Its use for treating inflammation was widespread. The Iroquois used a dandelion infusion to treat puffy eyes, whereas the Navajo used a poultice to treat swelling. The literature also makes mention of a curious use by the Iroquois for treating swollen testicles. I'll leave you to puzzle that one out.

Its use for inflammation could stem from a naturally-occurring chemical called quercetin found in dandelions, olives, apples, wine, and tea, among other sources. It is also an antioxidant. Some research suggest that it may increase mitochondrial content in muscle cells. Mitochondria are the energy power sources in the human body. And if it works, that could be a good thing.

Quercetin is an interesting chemical. Some medical evidence suggests that it can reduce mucus production induced by cigarette smoke. This action is one example of an acute immune system response. Chronic inflammation, on the other hand, is associated with atherosclerosis and arthritis. It certainly is something worth additional research.

Despite efforts to get rid of it, the dandelion has its own tricks. As you may have noticed in your own yard, it can interfere with the growth of plants growing near it. Part of the reason for that is because dandelion releases ethylene gas like conventional fruits and thus, may cause premature ripening in other plants that may compete for resources.

15 EVENING PRIMROSE

Common name: Evening Primrose

Other names: Common evening primrose, hoary evening primrose, fever plant, hooker evening primrose, coffee plant, sand lily

Scientific name: *Oenothera biennis*, Evening Primrose Family

Habitat: Dry to moderately dry prairies, disturbed sites

Season: Spring through fall

Status: Native

Type: Biennial/perennial forb

Identifying characteristics: Striking yellow blooms at the end of a slender stem, anywhere from 1 to 5 foot high.

Special cautions: The roots can be quite peppery, which might not be to everyone's taste. Do not ingest evening primrose if you are taking medication to control blood clotting.

Folklore

The name, evening primrose, refers to the fact that the flowers of this plant open in the evening when they are pollinated by insects active at twilight. During the latter part of summer, however, it will stay open during the day for a last chance at pollination.

Its genus name, *Oenothera*, comes from the Greek words, meaning wine hunt, though the precise reference is unknown. Some believe that it is said to increase the desire for drink, which may put you on the hunt for wine. Other stories say that it has the opposite effect.

The settlers and American Indians used evening primrose as a food staple. Many parts, after all, are edible. The Cherokee used the leaves as a cooked green. They also cooked the root, not unlike a potato or parsnip. The peppery taste of the roots tends to tame down toward the fall if your taste fall more along those lines. In addition to the other bits, the Gosiute people ate the seeds for food.

Its place in the pantry has some merit. The plant is nutritious and contains gamma-linoleinc acid (GLA), an essential fatty acid. Sunflower, hemp, and borage also contain GLA. The evening primrose is one of the few good sources.

However, the oil comes at a price since the seeds are very small, necessitating hand collection. You'll like find it as a dietary supplement, often blended with vitamin E.

The Iroquois had a couple of interesting uses for evening primrose. Because of its stimulant properties, it was thought to be a cure for laziness. In addition, they would rub the chewed roots on their arms to provide strength, and take care of any excuses for the laziness too.

Ecology: Minor value to wildlife. Evening primrose attracts moths that take advantage of its late hours.

Medicinal Use

The American Indians used evening primrose medicinally. The Ojibwa made a poultice of the entire plants for treating bruises. Its oil probably soothed all sorts of irritations. Science has confirmed its antimicrobial properties. The Potawatomi also used the plant as well, but what they did with it is unknown.

Settlers used it for a variety of purposes. Because of its antispasmodic properties, herbalists used evening primrose for treating whooping cough and asthma, using a syrup made from the flowers for this use. Its sedative and anti-inflammatory qualities from the GLA added to the relief it may have given.

On the other end of the spectrum, a tea made from evening primrose was said to cure obesity. The Cherokee also used it for this purpose. Even back in the day, people realized that being overweight wasn't good for your health and looked to Nature for cures.

Evening primrose oil is reputed to have several healing properties in the herbal medicine realm, including treatment for rosacea, nourishment for hair, and PMS prevention. Some dietary supplement manufacturers speak to these uses with commercial brands sold OTC.

Historical uses include treatment for migraines and even alcoholism, harking back to its wine hunt name. The literature also contains references to using it for other conditions, such as hyperactivity, hypertension, and hypercholesterolemia. Given its GLA content, the uses for hypertension and high cholesterol were not too far off base. I can't speak to the hyperactivity though.

Evening primrose may even have anti-aging potential for topical use because of its GLA content. In addition, it may have anticoagulant properties.

Because of these properties, you should not take it with aspirin, ginger, or any non-steroidal anti-inflammatory drugs like ibuprofen, which may act similarly. The same caution applies with any other anticoagulant medications you may be taking.

16 HEDGE BINDWEED

Common name: Hedge Bindweed

Other names: Hedge false bindweed, old man's night cap, devil's guts

Scientific name: *Calystegia sepium*, Morning Glory Family

Habitat: Prairies, meadows, disturbed areas

Season: Summer, fall

Status: Native

Type: Perennial vine

Identifying characteristics: Swallow-lobed, white trumpet-shaped flower with arrow-shaped leaves

Special cautions: All species in this family are mildly toxic. That's kind of like saying just a little poisonous. You were warned. It is considered a noxious weed in Texas and Arkansas, and thus, may be the target of pesticide applications.

Folklore

The species name for bindweed, *sepium*, is from the Latin word, sepes, meaning hedge. It is one of the most tenacious vines you'll likely ever encounter in the wild. This trait may have given rise to another of its common names, devil's guts. It is extremely hardy to boot, if it has entered the weed category in your world.

This legacy is ironic given its symbology for humility. Maybe it refers to a the hold on your affections or the fact that it rapidly gains its hold. In any case, it certainly would make an impression.

Hedge bindweed and its close relative field bindweed are members of the Morning Glory family, having similarly shaped blooms. The former will not open if the weather is poor, making it something of a weather forecaster in the realm of dandelion and chickweed. Field bindweed flowers are even known to close when it rains. But this applies only in the beginning of the season. Toward the end, they stay open even on moonlit nights to take advantage of the late season pollination.

Its various common names give you a clue to some of the folklore surrounding hedge bindweed. An old husband's tale says that if you want to kill bindweed you should unwind its twisted main stem and rewind it in the opposite direction. Its vine figures in other old stories as well.

The references to the devil belie its association with witches. It was said that witches used bindweed to bewitch an individual or just to capture her mind, anyway. Legend has it they would tie a vine around a figure representing the victim nine times. It was said to be especially potent if this the witch did this three days before the full moon.

But hedge bindweed also had more amiable uses. Legend has it that it could protect your home from intruders. It fits in with its magical uses for peace and happiness. Those associations may stem from its other historical uses. Back in the day, it was once used to add flavor to liqueurs, a potential cause for happiness of a sort.

Medicinal Use

All of the species of bindweed have similar medicinal properties, one of the most well-known being that of a purgative. Today we call it detoxing. In fact, some modern drugs for this purpose were developed using other members of its genus.

Despite of or maybe because of that trait, it was said that a tea made from the leaves and drunk before breakfast was an effective laxative. It was also known as a treatment for jaundice and gallbladder ailments. The latter may refer to the belief that it could increase the flow of bile.

The American Indians didn't use hedge bindweed extensively, but there were a few known historical uses. Its purgative properties were known to them as well. One accounts stated that hedge bindweed could act as an aid for handling rattlesnakes without harm if one rubbed it all one's body. Or at the very least, it could be used to tie up a snake —if given the opportunity.

17 INDIAN PIPE

Common name: Indian pipe

Other names: Ice plant, ghost plant, convulsion root

Scientific name: *Monotropa uniflora*, Indian Pipe Family

Habitat: Rich, shady forests

Season: Summer, fall

Status: Native

Type: Perennial forb

Identifying characteristics: White to dark stalk with scales and nodding top portion. Almost translucent appearing. Plant height is less than one foot tall

Special cautions: Possibly toxic as you may expect with a plant known as convulsion root.

Folklore

If there is one thing you can say about Indian pipe, it's that it's unlike any other plant you've seen before. With such a curious natural color, you'd think there would be many stories about Indian pipe. After all, finding a translucent white plant in the woods certainly would prove an unexpected sight, to be sure. But, it doesn't always stay white.

You can tell the relative age of a plant by its color as it darkens with age. It will also turn black if picked. These characteristics may have be the reason for the ghost plant moniker if nothing else.

Its scientific name is from the Latin meaning "one turn, one flower," in reference to its nodding head. Some say it lowers its head in shame at being associated with such wickedness and ghostly things.

It was said that an abundance of this plant meant that there would also be a lot of mushrooms, presumably because they thrive in similar conditions. Rich and moist forests provide the ideal habitat for these plants and fungi. I can certainly attest for the fact that when mushrooms are around, Indian pipe is sure to be too.

If a wild plant ever begged for a spooky association, Indian pipe has to be it. Its preferred habitat probably accounts for one of its other common names, corpse plant. It is said to be clammy to the touch and will turn black when handled. It's also known as ghost flower and ice plant. Its appearance in the fall not too long before Halloween must add to the folklore!

Food: Plant raw or cooked

Medicinal Use

Indian pipe served several functions in the folklore, many related to pain relief. These uses seem fitting, given the references to it as a possible opium substitute.

The Cherokee used the a plant concoction of its juice and water as a wash to relieve eye conditions and their associated discomforts. The Cree used it to take care of toothaches, while the Mohegan used it for pain associated with colds and fever.

A root tea was given to women after childbirth, adding to its history of pain relief use. The Potawatomi also used a tea as a *"female tonic."* The literature mentions its use for treating nervous conditions as well. Its sedative properties would account for this. Herbalists used it for a variety of nervous conditions, spasms, and fits. The Cherokee used it in similar ways as well as for treating convulsions in children, hence, the name convulsion root.

One has to wonder about any other magical uses it may have in association with these latter herbal remedies, given its features and color.

18 JACK IN THE PULPIT

Common name: Jack in the Pulpit

Other names: Indian jack in the pulpit, Indian turnip, devil's ear, dragon root, memory root, priest's pintle, bog onion

Scientific name: *Arisaema triphyllum*, Arum Family

Habitat: Rich woods, damp thickets

Season: Spring, summer

Status: Native

Type: Perennial forb

Identifying characteristics: Red-striped spathe that covers a green spadix. Divided leaf with three leaflets. Plant height is one to three feet tall

Special cautions: Jack in the pulpit contains calcium oxalate crystals in the berries, foliage, and roots of this plant, which will cause painful irritation of the mouth and throat if eaten raw. Some individuals may even have problems handling it. However, read on for a way around this unfortunate trait.

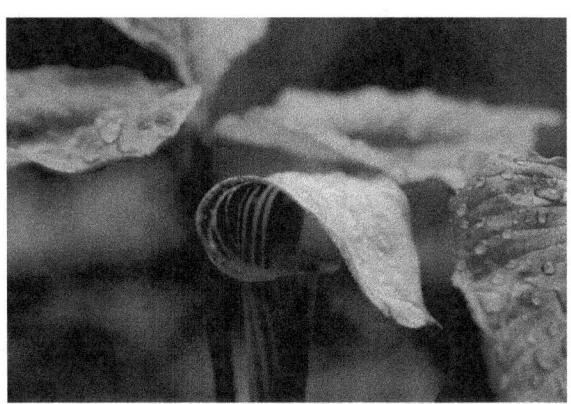

Folklore

Jack in the pulpit is an interesting plant, if just for its unusual shape. This may account for its curious list of other names like devil's ear and dragon root. The latter may refer to the literature's reference as it being "*brother to dragons.*" Or perhaps it refers to its pollinators, flies, and gnats, which get caught in its showy display.

Both male and female structures are present on the plants. The pulpit of its name refers to the arching spathe. Jack is the green spadix or spike where the flowers are present.

In her book, *Wildflowers Worth Noting*, Neltje Blanchan refers to it as a "*wolf in sheep's clothing, literally a 'brother to dragons.'*" Certainly, you must begin to wonder about a plant in which "Jack's whole aim in enticing visitors within his polished wall." But, as with any rumor, the morsels of truth point to the story. Our story begins with French explorer, Nicolas Perrot in the Upper Mississippi Valley in the mid-17th century.

Perrot wrote of its use by the Potawatomi. Because of the calcium oxalate crystals, it couldn't be eaten raw. However, they cooked and dried the plant and were able to convert this seemingly poisonous plant into an edible one. Drying was the only way. Boiling it would not take away its astringent nature.

The Potawatomi used the dried plant as a winter food. The dried root could also be ground for flour with a cocoa-like taste. Drying, however, takes several months. Consequently, they collected the plant in the spring. Jack in the pulpit typically shows up mid-spring.

While some sought to make it palatable, that wasn't always the case. Because it contains calcium oxalate, it had more sinister uses. The Meskwaki used it as a poison against enemies, either put on meat or in empty vessels for them to find and use.

It was also used for diagnostic purposes to predict either recovery or death. The latter use may refer to another of its unique characteristics. Jack in the pulpit has a disagreeable smell that attracts mosquitoes and perhaps flies. Despite this, historically, it was also a symbol of ardor and zeal.

Food: Dried root for seasoning; cooked root only; dried fruit seasoning on meat

Ecology: Eaten by pheasants and turkeys

Medicinal Use

Despite the cautions, Jack in the pulpit was used for medicinal purposes too. Curiously, a root poultice was used for treating sores. One can't help but wonder how putting something on a wound that can cause a burning sensation could help. Even more startling was its use by the Menominee as a treatment for sore eyes or the use by the Iroquois for treating listless babies.

The dried ground root was said to help digestion issues. Its analgesic properties made it a remedy for all sorts of pain, whether from headaches, sore joints, bruises, or cramps. Several nations used it as liniment for pain, including the Mohegan and Pawnee.

A poultice of the root was used to treat skin conditions. Again, you have to wonder about these uses too. Early settlers used the juice from the corm in a bit of lard for treating ringworm, a use also shared with the Cherokee. The calcium oxalate crystals may take your mind off the itching. It was commonly used as a poultice to treat inflammation and swelling. Some accounts mention its use as a remedy for snakebites.

Jack in the pulpit also was a contraceptive of sorts. Legend says that a teaspoon of the dried root in cold water could prevent pregnancy for a week. This use is just plain wrong. Caution was in order. If you took two teaspoons in hot water, you would become sterile—permanently.

19 JEWELWEED

Common name: Jewelweed

Other names: Touch-me-not, wild balsam, slipperweed

Scientific name: *Impatiens capensis*, Touch-Me-Not Family

Habitat: Moist forests and meadows

Season: Spring through fall

Status: Native

Type: Annual forb

Identifying characteristics: Orange or yellow tubular flowers. Stems fleshy and thick. Plant height is two to six feet tall

Special cautions: Berries can be toxic if eaten especially by children. It's often found in the same habitat as stinging nettle, so use caution when collecting. At least you'll have a remedy if you have an unpleasant brush with it. Jewelweed has strong emetic properties, so pass on the culinary uses.

Folklore

Jewelweed is unmistakable. It has thick succulent stem that contain a juice with verifiable medicinal value. I can personally vouch for its ability to "cure" stinging nettle pain. If there is one plant you should learn to identify, jewelweed is it. You can it growing in large stands in areas with moist soil—often close to the plants with the ill effect for which you may be seeking a cure.

As a food, the leaves can be boiled and eaten as a cooked green. But, like Jack in the pulpit, jewelweed contains calcium oxalate crystals. It should never be eaten raw. Its primary uses are more of a medicinal nature.

Ecology: Attracts hummingbirds

Medicinal Use

The most common use for jewelweed was for treating skin ailments from poison ivy and stinging nettle to burns to insect bites. Coincidentally and fortunately, jewelweed usually occurs in the same habitat as stinging nettle. This use was shared by the Omaha, Cherokee and Meskwaki, to name a few. Its sap provides quick and soothing relief.

This quality made it effective for treating other skin conditions uses, such as burns, bruises, and even liver spots. In addition, the Penobscot used an ointment made from the buds and rum to treat cuts. Other historical uses include a treatment for sprains, ringworm, and warts.

Herbalists used the leaves in a tea for treating fever and the measles. It was also a cure for stomach complaints and cramps. Several cultures, including the Micmac, used it as a liver aid. It was used into the modern age for treating dropsy and jaundice.

The literature also mentions a use of a stem concoction to be given to women in childbirth, which makes sense given its other useful purposes. With other common names such as lady's eardrops and silver cap, you knew there had to be some stories.

20 MAY APPLE

Common name: May Apple

Other names: Indian apple, wild mandrake, hog apple, raccoon berry, wild lemon, duck's foot, umbrella plant

Scientific name: *Podophyllum peltatum*, Barberry Family

Habitat: Moist woods

Season: Spring

Status: Native

Type: Perennial forb

Identifying characteristics: White flowers located below the deep-lobed leaves. Yellow fruit. Fragrant. Plant height is one to two feet tall

Special cautions: The unripe fruit and its leaves are poisonous. Sometimes the ripe fruit is too. May apple is listed as endangered in Florida, so definitely avoid collecting it there.

Folklore

While may apple is also known as mandrake, it is not the same plant as the mandrake found in Europe. Its genus name, *Podophyllum*, literally means foot leaf, a reference to one of its other common names, duck foot.

Its historical uses range from the innocent to the malevolent. The Delaware used may apple as a love charm. Other nations thought differently about it. The Iroquois used it as medicine to increase strength. And like many wild plants, may apple has its quirky side.

One old husband's tale says that if a girl plucks up the root of the plant, she will become pregnant. The literature doesn't mention how this would happen. But the stories don't end here.

Like cinquefoil, may apple has associations with witches. It was called "witches umbrella" back in the day. The collective shape of the leaves does indeed resemble a brolly, so it wasn't too much of a stretch.

Another common name for may apple is green umbrellas said to open during April showers, again referring back to the umbrella-shaped leaves. These rains hastened the ripening of the may apples, hence, its name. In any case, it is one of the earlier and perhaps more showy of the spring wildflowers.

But despite its whimsical association with spring, it was said to be a powerful addition to a deadly witch's brew. The toxicity of the plants bears this out. It was considered a poison by several American Indian nations.

The literature contains references to the fruit as an insecticide particularly for potatoes, in keeping with the toxic tradition. While the Menominee didn't eat it, they boiled the plants to get a poison for killing potato bugs, taking advantage of its lethal quality.

Food: While the ripe fruit is edible for the most part, the rest of the plant is highly toxic despite the fact that animals eat it with no ill effect. Nevertheless, many American Indian nations used the fruit as a staple food.

Medicinal Use

May apple is not a plant for the beginning herbalist. It is a powerful plant that has cathartic and purgative properties, albeit, slow acting. Settlers used the plant for digestive complaints, perhaps thinking it would be best to rid one of the poison—literally.

It is also a powerful intestinal stimulant. Historically, herbalists used may apple to treat liver ailments and venereal disease, undoubtedly because of these qualities. I suppose it acted as another way to scare the Devil out of you.

The root of the plants was used in different forms to treat sores and deafness. The literature also makes mention of soaking the root in whiskey to relieve muscle pain, though perhaps the whiskey alone could probably do that much. It was also used for a variety of other digestive ills. William Bartram, the 19th century American naturalist, documented its use by American Indians for treating intestinal worms.

Science has supported some of the medicinal uses of may apple. The leaves contain an ingredient called podophyllotoxin, which has been used for treating lung and testicular cancers. It may also have some efficacy for use to remove benign skin growths.

Commercially, this compound was derived from plants from the Himalayas that are now endangered. Researchers are investigating the possibility of cultivating may apples for production of this medicine.

Other possible medicinal uses comes from one of its constituents called quercetin, which dandelions also contain. This compound is an antioxidant that has anti-inflammatory properties, including the ability to reduce histamine release.

Scientific research has shown some promise for its use for treating asthma as a bronchodilator. Because of these properties, you should avoid ingesting plants that contain quercetin if you are taking antibiotics or have asthma.

21 MILKWEED

Common name: Milkweed

Other names: Silkweed, butterfly weed, wild cotton, cotton weed

Scientific name: *Asclepias syriaca*, Milkweed Family

Habitat: Dry to wet meadows, prairies and fields

Season: Summer

Status: Native

Type: Perennial forb

Identifying characteristics: Cream to pink-colored umbel flowers with large, rough pods. Plant height is three to six feet tall

Special cautions: On the down side, milkweed is potentially toxic and emetic in large doses. It is toxic to poultry, so keep the chickens out of it. As with other wetland plants, beware of the other ones that may share the habitat.

Folklore

Milkweed is probably best known for its association with monarch butterflies. Milkweed contains ingredients called cardiac glycosides, which makes the larvae and adults toxic to birds. But they are not the only ones. Grazing animals tend to avoid it for good reason. Ingestion of large quantities of milkweed can be poisonous to them as well.

Despite these negative qualities, it is a useful plant for humans both as food and medicine. The pods and shoots are edible. You can tame the bitter taste of the leaves and stems with boiling.

The American Indians used milkweed primarily as a food source. The Ojibwa, Potawatomi and Menominee all used the shoots and flowers, often as an addition to a meat-based broth. It has a gelatinous quality like okra when cooked, making it a possible thickener. The young shoots were also eaten like asparagus. In addition, the Menominee dried and stored it as a winter food source.

Then, there is the characteristic seeds that can be used for fiber. The plant lent itself to other uses, perhaps only rivaling the cattail in its versatility. The Cherokee, for example, used its plant fibers from the inner bark of the stems to make bowstrings. It was also used to make fishing lines. The seed floss makes a good stuffing material for pillows and the like.

On the other end of the spectrum, the Chippewa and Ojibwa used the root of the plant for calling in deer when hunting. It was said to imitate the call of a young fawn.

From an artistic perspective, it is hard to deny the beauty of the split pod with its silky seeds bursting forth and ready to take to the wind! It is a classic still life subject.

Medicinal Use

Its genus name, *Asclepias*, is from the Greek god of healing, Asklepios. Herbalists used a root tea for a variety of purposes, including as a laxative, a heart tonic, and asthma remedy. These uses make sense considering its digitalis-like properties. However, that also makes it more dangerous to use without the proper knowledge.

Its name may also give you an indication of another use. The Chippewa made a decoction of its root to encourage the flow of milk in lactating women. The Quebec and Mohawk, on the other hand, used it as a contraceptive, albeit a dangerous one. Like Jack in the pulpit, some believed it could cause temporary sterility.

The sap had other uses. Rubbed on the skin, it could treat warts and ringworm. Speaking of skin conditions, the Iroquois used it to treat bee stings and cuts as well. Milkweed was used to provide relief from chest discomfort, backaches, or rheumatism. The roots have diuretic and sedative qualities that can account for some of its uses.

Scientific research has found that milkweed contains flavonoid compounds. These organic substances have found to inhibit the formation of blood clots, according to a 2012 study by the Beth Israel Deaconess Medical Center.

22 MOONSEED

Common name: Moonseed

Other names: Vine maple, moonseed sarsaparilla

Scientific name: *Menispermum canadense*, Moonseed Family

Habitat: Moist woods and thickets

Season: Summer

Status: Native

Type: Perennial vine

Identifying characteristics: Low-lying vine with maple-like leaves. The fruit forms bunches like grapes, though with fewer fruits.

Special cautions: The black fruit, which resembles the edible wild grape, is highly toxic and potentially fatal if eaten.

Folklore

This is another example of a plant that makes correct identification imperative. Its name refers to the moon shape of its seeds. The leaves and fruit resemble wild grape—and presumably, the moon. Unlike wild grape, moonseed is not edible and quite the contrary.

You'll need everything you need to know by looking at the plant's leaves. While grape has toothed leaves, moonseed has smooth edges on its leaves. It also has no tendrils. To complicate matters more, the two plants often grow in the same environment, often alongside each other.

Because of its toxicity, I included moonseed more as a PSA than as a plant with a long and varied history of folklore applications. Despite the silence there, American Indians used it medicinally.

Medicinal Use

Despite its toxicity, moonseed was used for medicinal purposes though it had a lot going against it. It tastes bitter. It could act as a purgative or laxative, not exactly the medicine that you'd like to take.

Nevertheless, herbalists used the root for treating digestion complaints and inflammation. The Delaware, on the other hand, used it topically for treating sores. The literature also mentions its use as a blood cleanser and diuretic. There are other accounts of it being used as tonic or stimulant. Though it was used by the Ojibwa, its precise purpose is unknown.

The Cherokee considered it a stimulant to be taken by "*weakly females.*" Its bitter taste certainly would make anyone sit up and notice. It was also used by them to treat nausea and venereal diseases. Given its other qualities, it seems unlikely that it could provide much comfort.

In fact, there may be some potential for moonseed for medical use. The plant contains an alkaloid called dauricine. An alkaloid is a nitrogen-containing organic compound. Common examples include morphine and quinine. The alkaloid in moonseed has shown potential for preventing and possibly treating breast and colon cancers.

23 MULLEIN

Common name: Mullein

Other names: Flannel plant, hag's taper, velvet dock, Quaker's rouge, candle wick, feltwort, Juniper's staff, wild tobacco

Scientific name: *Verbascum thapsus*, Figwort Family

Habitat: Disturbed sites

Season: Summer

Status: Introduced

Type: Biennial forb

Identifying characteristics: Basal rosette of thick, fleshy leaves in first year plants. Tall stalk with yellow flower in the second year. Plant height is one to six feet tall. A stand of mullein is a remarkable sight.

Special cautions: The seeds are toxic, providing another example of a plant with edible and non-edible parts. It is considered a noxious weed in Colorado and Hawaii, so there's also the risk of pesticide contamination. Then, there is the leaves. They contain coumarin, an anticoagulant. You should use this one with extreme caution. And you should avoid consuming if you take a daily aspirin or blood thinner medication.

Folklore

A plant that inspired American naturalist and nature essayist, John Burroughs, to pen,

"I have come three thousand miles to see the mullein cultivated in a garden, and christened the velvet plant,"

…is certainly is worthy of some notice. Like many non-native plants, mullein found its way accidentally to North America. And it's no wonder.

With over 40 folks names inspired by its curative properties among other uses, settlers certainly would have wanted mullein in the New World. You might find references to mullein as old man's flannel, Peter's staff, clown's lugwort, rag paper, and beggar's blanket, among many others. And you know that each of them has a story.

Mullein has two forms, depending upon the stage in its life cycle. It begins as a low-growing and modest-looking rosette. During its second year, it will grow the characteristic long taper that can reach heights up to six feet, sometimes more. The latter stage probably provides the most inspiration for the folk names for this common plant.

This plant has a long history of magical and mystical associations that may make you rethink how you feel about it. The form of mullein and its characteristics made it a subject of stories of witches and mischief. Legend has it that witches used mullein as wicks in their candles to cast their spells.

It was said to ward off evil spirits and for rites such as divination and exorcism. These associations may explain why they were used as funeral torches during the Middle Ages.

And if you planted it on a Sunday with other plants of protection such as violets or marigolds, you could be protected from evil spirits. It also has an association with the planet, Saturn, based on Nicholas Culpepper's 17th century astrological classification of plants.

Culpepper was a 17th century English botanist and astrologer. His book, *Astrological Judgment of Diseases from the Decumbiture of the Sick* provides a guide to the use of astrology in medicine. With their associations to mythology, herbalists of the day used many common plants like mullein for treating the ill.

If nightmares or demons disturbed your sleep, a white bag filled with mullein leaves placed under your pillow could ensure a restful slumber.

Mullein was said to be sacred to the supreme Roman deity, Jupiter. Talk about friends in high places. With Pagans, it was considered a sacred plant, used to cleanse ritual tools and altars.

The Hopi smoked the leaves as an anti-convulsive for treating fits and witchcraft. Other peoples smoked mullein ceremonially, including the Isleta. Curiously, it was also used historically as a remedy to stop smoking.

Its seemingly magical properties don't end here. The Navajo used an infusion to increase strength both in hunters and horses. The Ojibwa used it similarly as a heart stimulant. Because of its collection of uses, it is hard to think that this plant is anything but valuable. And it didn't matter who was using it.

It was said that mullein was also used by poachers. It was also reputed to protect against wild animals, though it would seem as if the animals were more in need of the protecting. The irritating nature of the down covering of the plant may explain this claim rather than any mystical powers.

Poachers seemed to have no end of uses for it. They would feed the seeds to fish with the thought that it would intoxicate them and make for easy pickings.

There are several early accounts in Europe of it being used as a fish poison because of its narcotic properties, so it might have indeed worked. The plant does contain rotenone, which is a broad-spectrum pesticide and piscicide, i.e., fish killer.

You won't find rotenone available commercially anymore in the United States and Canada. And the World Health Organization considers it mildly hazardous. Don't say that you weren't warned.

Despite all of this, mullein has a kinder and gentler nature too. It was said that if you could attract the attention of the opposite sex if you carried a mullein leaf with you. This use may be related to another of its purported uses.

The common name, Quaker's rouge, refers to a story that Quaker girls would rub the rough leaves of the mullein on their cheeks to color them. The effect was caused by an allergic reaction to the hairs of the leaves. The things we do for love!

Ecology: Attracts bees and butterflies

Medicinal Use

Mullein is one wild plant that has made it from the meadow to the store shelves despite what the WHO has to say about it. You can find it as a dietary supplement, a tea, and as eardrops. It may improve the health of mucous membranes.

Most of the folklore uses for mullein involve respiratory issues. A leaf decoction treated colds or a sore throat. Some herbalists used mullein as an inhalant for treating tonsil inflammation. In addition, the literature mentions its use for treating tuberculosis.

As its moniker, wild tobacco, would lead you to believe, American Indians smoked mullein leaves. The surprising thing was that it was used for respiratory ailments. The Potawatomi smoked the dried leaves for treating asthma, which strikes me as an odd application. They would also smudge the leaves to revive someone who had fainted.

Because of its unpleasant taste, the Cherokee mixed it with honey for treating coughs. The Navajo, on the other hand, countered the taste by mixing it with regular tobacco for use in treating mental disorders.

But American Indians also used it to treat disease. It was used to treat a variety of other respiratory illnesses, including mumps, consumption, and croup. These uses have persisted into modern times. Perhaps there is some truth to the stories after all. Mullein is approved for use in Germany for congestion and coughs.

A poultice was said to relieve irritated mucous membranes due to its anti-inflammatory and emollient properties. The plant is also a diuretic and anti-bacterial agent. These factors contributed to its use for treating cuts, wounds, and even for relieving pain in teething babies.

In fact, mullein had numerous uses in this regard that harken back to its anti-inflammatory properties. Some used in for other irritating conditions like chapped lips to splinters to chilblains to hemorrhoids.

Its use as a tea goes back as well. Some herbalists made a tea from mullein for digestive issues as well as other diverse uses, including blood purifier and treatment for swelling. The Iroquois even used it to treat a baby's broken coccyx, should the poor child be so afflicted.

The mention of tuberculosis is particularly interesting. Because of its expectorant properties, it was used as a treatment for this condition. Research has confirmed that it does indeed have strong anti-TB potential as well as anti-viral activity.

24 OX-EYE DAISY

Common name: Ox-eye daisy

Other names: Common daisy, oxeye daisy, field daisy

Scientific name: *Leucanthemum vulgare*, Aster Family

Habitat: Fields, disturbed sites

Season: Spring through fall

Status: Introduced

Type: Perennial forb

Identifying characteristics: White petals with a yellow to orange-yellow disk flower in the center. Plant height up to two feet tall

Special cautions: The ox-eye daisy may cause dermatitis in some individuals, especially if you are allergic to ragweed. Unfortunately, it's not all buttercups and daisies with daises.

It can produce an off flavor in milk if dairy cattle consume it, so it's not welcome in the pasture. Finally, it is considered a noxious weed in Colorado, Montana, Ohio, Washington, and Wyoming. Take care when collecting because of the possibility of pesticide exposure if you find it.

Folklore

The genus name for the ox-eye daisy, *Leucanthemum*, comes from the Greek for "white flower." Its species name, *vulgare*, is Latin for common. It has nothing to do with its manners or taste in bad jokes.

The ox-eye daisy is well known in Europe, where in Scotland it is known as 'bairnwort," meaning child flower in reference to the daisy chains children would make with it. It was said to keep fairies from one's yard and snatching away children. On the other hand, if young women wore a chain of them on their heads, it could attract their beloved.

It's hard to believe that this sweet little flower is considered a weed, especially given some of its other associations. An old Christian name for the ox-eye daisy was "Maudlinwort" after Mary Magdalen. Deities of all sorts revered it. It was said to be sacred to the Greek goddess, Artemis and Thor, the Norse god of thunder.

If you wanted to grow a garden for love, you should plant daisies on a Friday any time when the moon is not waning since this is the day of Venus. You could plant it with other plants associated with love, including pansy, tulip, and geranium. In the language of flowers, the daisy symbolizes innocence and purity.

Another common name is "day's eye," which refers to the fact that it closes at night. It has a history as being a harbinger of spring, where in England it was said that spring had not yet arrived unless you stepped on 12 daisies. Don't ask me why 12. Other numbers like 7 or 10 are perfectly good numbers too.

Of course, there is also its association with love. "He loves me. He loves me not." Here's a tip. Since most plants have an uneven number of leaves, you should start with the former to get the answer you want.

Legend has it that the daisy could repel lightning. For this reason, it was hung in homes to protect them. If you hung them on Midsummer's Eve, it would bring the blessing of fairies. Sometimes, you wanted the fairies' attention and sometimes not.

While the leaves were eaten, the root was believed to stunt your growth. A concoction with milk was sometimes given to animals. In the language of dreams, to envision walking in a field of daisies was a good thing. You could expect help from someone.

That's if you dream about it at the right time. Woe to you, however, should you dream of them out of season. This was a warning of some hidden evil in your life.

Food: Young tender leaves, shoots, and root can be added to a salad.

Medicinal Use

The daisy has a long history of folklore use. Some of its main uses include a treatment for wounds as well as for aches and pains, perhaps caused by the wounds. Another common name for the ox-eye daisy is bruisewort in a nod to this use. It was said to be a treatment for battle wounds in the field during the Middle Ages. The word, "wort" comes from the Old English wyrt, meaning root or plant.

Herbalists of many cultures also used daisies a treatment for scurvy or spring tonic. Both the Europeans and some American Indian cultures such as the Mohegan used it this way.

But, like all good stories, there is a kernel of truth. It has some nutritional value as a source of vitamins A and C as well as calcium and iron. It may have provided some relief.

But other stories may leave you wondering. Because of its association with Venus, it was believed to be good for wounds in the breast. Yes, a bit of reach if you ask me too.

The ox-eye daisy was not used extensively by American Indians with some exceptions. The Menominee used it to treat fevers. The European settlers used it too. The literature mentions that it is an effective treatment for whooping cough and asthma, making the use for fevers plausible. In addition, the ox-eye daisy has diuretic and anti-spasmodic properties.

25 PURPLE CONEFLOWER

Common name: Purple coneflower

Other names: Snakeroot, echinacea, scurvy root, prairie coneflower

Scientific name: *Echinacea purpurea*, Aster Family

Habitat: Dry to moderately dry prairies and woods

Season: Spring through fall

Status: Native

Type: Perennial forb

Identifying characteristics: Pale pink to deep pink-lavender petals that droop downward away from the spiked seed head. Plant height is two to five feet tall

Special cautions: The purple coneflower is endangered in Florida and probably extirpated in Michigan. It is off limits in these states. It is also becoming rare in some areas due to over-collecting because of medicinal value. Think carefully before you decide to collect it.

Despite some compelling evidence, you should not use echinacea for long-term use as it may suppress your immune system. Take care when collecting and using purple coneflower if you have allergies to plants in the Aster family, such as ragweed. It may cause a similar reaction.

Folklore

Its genus name, *Echinacea*, comes from the Greek word, echino, meaning hedgehog or sea urchin. You'll think it's an apt description by its prickly seed head. But, then again, it might be a metaphor for its hardy nature.

It is a native prairie plant that is drought-resistant. And it would be too. Like many prairie plants, it grows an extensive root system, reaching down over 10 feet. Its ability to self-sow and reproduce quickly make it a good addition for a native plant garden.

Ecology: Attracts butterflies, hummingbirds, and a variety of natural pollinators and birds looking for its nutritious seeds. Though some claim it is deer-resistant, the deer in my backyard didn't get that memo. Neither did the geese.

Medicinal Use

Echinacea has a strong reputation as an effective preventive for colds and flu. The first pharmaceutical preparations came into the market in 1895.

It was widely used before antibiotics became commonplace. It was the fifth best-selling herbal supplements in 2009, with sales over $16 million. This is almost a seven percent increase since 2008. Cold and flue, after all, are big business.

There are over 200 pharmaceutical preparations made from echinacea available in Germany alone. The German Commission E lists colds, fevers, and coughs among its many applications for it. Of all the plants in this collection, purple coneflower stands unique in its accepted and approved use in some areas.

Historically, it was not used as extensively as today's popularity may indicate, though its use was widespread among American Indians. The Choctaw used the root to treat coughs. The literature also contains references to a root tea for stimulating immune system. The Delaware and Oklahoma peoples used a root infusion for treating venereal disease.

Echinacea has both antibacterial and fungicidal properties that may have made it effective. As a natural antibiotic, it can promote healing with its cortisone-like activity and anti-bacterial properties.

Echinacea also stimulates immune system cells to produce virus-fighting substances. While it cannot cure a cold, it can lessen its duration and severity. It remains a good example of a wild plant that has found a place in the modern pharmacy.

26 PUSSY TOES

Common name: Pussy toes

Other names: Cat's foot, field pussy toes, prairie everlasting

Scientific name: *Antennaria neglecta*, Aster Family

Habitat: Dry to moderately moisture woods and prairies, lawns

Season: Spring, summer

Status: Native

Type: Perennial forb

Identifying characteristics: White to pinkish dense flowers at end of stems up to 16 inches tall. Leaves are hairy, with basal leaves hairless

Special cautions: Since pussy toes had some use in midwifery, pregnant women should avoid using it. This caution comes from my own assessment of its history, rather than a specific scientific reference.

Folklore

What's not to like about a plant named pussy toes? If for no other reason than its adorable name is pussy toes in this book. But it also has some positive associations for me.

For the Upper Midwest, it is a good plant to know, especially if you collect morels in the spring. When violets and pussy toes pop up, the morels are likely around too.

Its species name, *neglecta*, means neglected in Latin, so sad for a plant with such a lovely name. Historically, pussy toes was used for a variety of domestic purposes, most notably to get rid of pests. A shampoo made from the flower heads would take care of lice. It was also packed with one's winter's clothes to keep away moths.

Otherwise, the literature is silent about it. I included it because it is one of my favorite wild plants. While this species was not used extensively, a similar species called Howell's pussy toes was also known as ladies tobacco.

Medicinal Use

Pussy toes had varied uses in the folklore. Herbalists used it to treat coughs and colds. A tea made from the plant was said to treat respiratory ailments. The Ojibwa made a tea from the entire plant that was given to women after childbirth to expel the afterbirth. Other medicinal uses in the folklore include a remedy for rattlesnake bites and a poultice for bruises.

27 QUEEN ANNE'S LACE

Common name: Queen Anne's lace

Other names: Wild carrot, bird's nest, devil's plaque

Scientific name: *Daucus carota*, Carrot Family

Habitat: Disturbed sites, roadsides

Season: Summer

Status: Introduced

Type: Biennial forb

Identifying characteristics: White umbel with numerous blooms that has the characteristic red to red-purple dot in the center. Plant height is one to five feet tall

Special cautions: Queen Anne's lace closely resembles water hemlock, a highly poisonous plant. It is a vital lesson in the importance of proper identification. Nevertheless, it is considered a noxious weed in Iowa, Michigan, Ohio, and Washington. If the poison isn't within the plant, it may be sprayed onto it.

Folklore

Like many plants, Queen Anne's lace has both medicinal and culinary value. How could it not with such a regal name?

It is highly nutritious, providing a good source of a variety of vitamins and minerals, including niacin, pantothenic acid, and magnesium.

Several American Indian nations used it for food, including the Kitasoo and Oweekeno peoples. Some stored the dried fruit as a winter food staple. Considering its nutritional value, storing it through the cold months probably wasn't a bad idea.

Its genus name, *Daucus*, comes from the Greek word, dais, meaning to burn. If you look close, you'll see that it has a red dot in the center of the plant that makes it a subject of folklore.

One account says that it is a drop of blood from the queen who pricked her finger while making lace. Another legends states that the center flower is a cure for epilepsy. With only one red flower in a cluster of white, you know there must be something special about it.

As one of its common names would imply, it does have a carrot-like odor. Its species name, *carota*, comes from the Greek word, daukos, which means carrot, hence, the name, wild carrot.

Another common name, devil's plague, is in reference to how difficult this plant can be to control because it is so prolific. If you love it as I do, you'll be in good company with the flies, bees, and wasps that enjoy it too. That may explain its dubious classification as a noxious weed in some states.

The ancient Greeks revered Queen Anne's lace, saving it for specific uses. Crowns made from the plant were worn by the victors of the Grecian games. Another account states they were place on the graves of loved ones, to assure the departed that they are still remembered.

It was thought to be an antidote for poison. As a gesture of kindness and trust to a dinner guest, a sprig of the plant was placed on the guest's plate. One can't help but wonder why the thought of being poisoned might cross a guest's mind in the first place. Whatever its value, it was considered bad luck to transplant it.

Food: Seeds eaten fresh or dried; cooked root; fried flowers

Ecology: Minor value to birds and small mammals

Medicinal Use

From a medicinal point of view, Queen Anne's lace has enormous potential. Historically, herbalists made a tea for treating inflammation. Science has confirmed this, along with antihistaminic and immunostimulant activity.

Historically, herbalists used it to treat a kidney diseases and digestive disorders. It was reputed to be an effective cure for dropsy, due to its diuretic properties.

While both men and women were given Queen Anne's lace, the Iroquois had several treatments specifically for men. A decoction of roots remedied blood disorders, loss of appetite, and even acne in men. The Mohegan used an infusion for diabetes or low blood sugar. Other uses include a root poultice for treating sores. Its historical topical use explains its contemporary use in perfumes and anti-wrinkle creams.

Queen Anne's lace has been the subject of much scientific research, particularly with cancer treatment. For example, a study by Lebanese American University found that wild carrot oil demonstrated remarkable anti-tumor activity against skin cancer.

Another study by Sheffield Hallam University in the United Kingdom found its juice extracts inhibited the proliferation of leukemia. Both studies remarked on the wild carrot's excellent potential for developing cancer treatments.

Science has also confirmed that it has hypotensive properties. This is probably due to the fact that it is a diuretic and can help reduce blood volume. And lower blood volume means that your heart has to work less to get your blood circulating throughout your body.

However, because of this trait, individuals being treated for high blood pressure should refrain from ingesting Queen Anne's lace because of the possibility of interfering with your medication.

Likewise, pregnant women should also avoid it. It can cause uterine contractions. Some reports mention it as a "morning after" remedy because of this effect.

28 SPIDERWORT

Common name: Spiderwort

Other names: Common spiderwort, blue-jacket, smooth spiderwort

Scientific name: *Tradescantia ohiensis*, Spiderwort Family

Habitat: Dry to moderately dry prairies and meadows

Season: Spring, summer

Status: Native

Type: Perennial forb

Identifying characteristics: Flower with three purple to blue-purple petals. Leaves are blade like. Plant height is one to three feet tall

Special cautions: n/a

Folklore

I included spiderwort because it is a striking plant, even if the literature doesn't have a lot to say about it. Wherever you spot it, spiderwort is sure to catch your eye, if just because of its truly beautiful purple color.

It has the appearance of an orchid, delicate and beautiful in its simplicity. In the language of flowers, spiderwort means respect, but not romantic love.

In mythology, it is associated with Venus and Aphrodite despite the lack of romance. It may instead refer to its delicate nature. "*When touched in the heat of the day, the flowers shrivel to a fluid jelly.*"

Food: Leaves can be eaten as part of a salad or a cooked green. The flowers can be candied.

Ecology: Important for bees

Medicinal Use

Its name, spiderwort, literally means spider plant. This may be a reference to its historical use for treating skin rashes, some perhaps caused by spiders. Some American Indians used a poultice made from the crushed leaves for this purpose as well as stings or other insect bites.

A root tea was also used to treat several types of ailments, including digestive issues, kidney ailments and female miscellaneous problems. Take note about this use, Ladies.

29 SWEET FLAG

Common name: Sweet flag

Other names: Calamus

Scientific name: *Acorus americanus*, Calamus Family

Habitat: Marshes, shallow ponds

Season: Spring, summer

Status: Native

Type: Perennial forb

Identifying characteristics: Aromatic when leaves are bruised

Special cautions: Hands off in Pennsylvania. It is an endangered plant here. And as with other wetland plants, use caution when collecting in areas that may have stinging nettle, snakes, and other nasties.

Folklore

American Indians have revered and used sweet flag historically more so than Europeans. The Cheyenne, for example, believed that sweet flag was a powerful medicine.

A bit of root tied to a child's clothing was said to ward off the night spirits and ghosts. The Iroquois used sweet flag for detecting bewitchment so a suitable treatment could be then applied.

Other cultures ascribed it as a hunting medicine. The Chippewa used a root decoction on their fishing nets. Hunting deer or fish, sweet flag was a go-to plant.

Other peoples used it too but for very different reasons. The plant has hallucinogenic effects, which explains why the root was chewed by some peoples. It was also used in ceremonies and for trade perhaps for just that reason.

Medicinal Use

Sweet flag was an important medicinal plant for American Indians. One of its main uses was for treating stomach cramps and indigestion. Only a very small bit was necessary, which is fortunate given its bitter taste.

Settlers used the plant as well, but found a way around its unpleasantness. They would make candied slices with sweet flag to make the medicine go down easier. It's called sweet for a reason.

The Potawatomi used sweet flag as part of a cure to stop a hemorrhage. Mixed with arbor vitae and shining willow, the mixture was boiled and reduced. A tablespoon was administered every hour until the bleeding stopped. Similarly, the Shinnecock believed that the chewed root could "dry your blood."

Sweet flag was used to treat pain of all sorts, from headaches to chest pain to abdominal cramps. To the Cheyenne, it was more a panacea, with the root rubbed on the skin to cure any ailment.

Many other cultures viewed it similarly. Most times it was eaten. However, the Winnebago took the cure one step further by injecting it with a bird wing bone for general health.

It had widespread use for treating several common ailments such as colds and toothaches. Though some Indian nations used it to treat gonorrhea, it has been found to have weak to no anti-microbial activity against this condition.

But there's bad news too. Sweet flag contains chemicals considered carcinogenic. Because of this fact, the FDA banned sweet flag as a food additive. Distillers still use it, however. They apparently took Paracelsus's advice about doses literally.

30 TANSY

Common name: Tansy

Other names: Common tansy, garden tansy, golden buttons, stinking Willie, parsley fern

Scientific name: *Tanacetum vulgare*, Aster Family

Habitat: Disturbed sites, roadsides

Season: Summer

Status: Introduced

Type: Perennial forb

Identifying characteristics: Clusters of dense yellow flowers. Hairless, feather-like leaves. Aromatic. Plant height is one to five feet tall

Special cautions: The concentrated oil is highly toxic and potentially fatal. It may also cause dermatitis, but that would be a non-issue in some cases.

And as if that weren't enough, tansy can cause miscarriages. Perhaps for these reasons and its invasive nature, it is considered a noxious weed in Colorado, Montana, Washington, and Wyoming.

Folklore

Tansy is an extremely tolerant and hardy plant, able to grow even in less than ideal conditions. These characteristics undoubtedly gave rise to its name which comes from the Greek word "athanasia" meaning immortality. The Greek mythology mentions that the divine hero, Ganymede, was given it so that he would be immortal. The name, tansy, seems an appropriate moniker given this association.

Most wild plants have a plethora of uses and generally are not restricted to a particular ailment. Tansy is no exception. On the practical side, the attractive yellow flowers of tansy make a pretty dye, while the young shoots make a delicate green hue.

It is native to parts of Europe and Asia, where it was widely used for culinary purposes. You'll find many tasty references to tansy, including tansy teas, tansy cakes, and tansy puddings.

Given its toxic nature, these references seem curious. Equally odd is the lack of other names pointing to its dark side. Perhaps tansy is a literal example of the dose that Paracelsus referred to.

The aromatic plant has an interesting scent that lent itself to a unique flavoring for foods. Perhaps this explains why the Ojibwa burned the flowers to attract deer when hunting. It may have worked!

Tansy also had a religious significance, being one of the plants dedicated to the Virgin Mary in the 16th century. The literature also refers its connection to Easter. After the ordeal of Lent, one would eat a tansy cake as a means of purification.

Tansy had other religious connections. It was traditionally associated with the Pagan Sabbath of the Spring Equinox. Tansy was also believed to provide protection against monsters when hung on one's house, back in the day when the devil could be blamed for any sort of dark deed.

The opposite, however, is a more accurate description. The concentrated oil is highly toxic and part of the FDA poisonous plant database. It is forbidden to sell it in the United States.

A less sinister historical use was as an insect repellent, which is undoubtedly due to its odor not unlike camphor. An old husband's tale claims that it repels flies and ants. The plant contains thujone, which is an pesticide and accounts in part for its toxicity.

Medicinal Use

Despite its toxic nature, tansy served a diverse collection of purposes. It was widely used and available to American colonists. A tea from the root of the plant was used to treat digestive issues. It was considered a tonic that could treat exhaustion, ingestion, or hysteria.

Another account calls for its use as a plant steam bath for sore feet and inflammation. These uses make it sound like something that would be in any settler's medicine chest.

One of its principle uses, however, was to rid children of worms, a practice used by settlers and some American Indian nations, including the Cherokee. Given its poisonous nature, you have to wonder how effective it really was. Equally curious is the fact that herbalists used it to induce abortions.

Like many wild plants, tansy had strong associations of a female nature. Some American Indians believed that it could prevent miscarriages if worn around the waist or in one's shoes. Other cultures such as the Malecite used it as contraception. Still other sources mention its use for menstrual irregularities. Whether true or not, it is for this reasons that tansy is not recommended for use by pregnant women.

But it has its good side too. The folklore contains many references to the use of tansy for relieving pain, whether it was caused by sciatica or other pains inside your body. It could treat skin conditions, such as acne and sunburn. It was even believed that it was a remedy to "fasten loose teeth."

Scientific research has uncovered a diverse collection of possible medicinal uses for tansy. A study by the Russian Academy of Sciences, for example, found it has a protective effect against *Escherichia coli*. This discovery is especially important in light of the fact that more antibiotic-resistant strains have been occurring.

Other research has found that tansy possess anti-leukemic properties. Though probably not a use you may need ordinarily, another study that it has potential for use as a snakebite anti-venom against the king cobra bites. In any case, the cautions associated with using tansy are numerous and not to be taken lightly.

31 TRILLIUM

Common name: Trillium

Other names: White wake-robin, white trillium, Indian turnip, stinking Benjamin, trinity plant

Scientific name: *Trillium grandiflorum*, Lily Family

Habitat: Rich forests and thickets

Season: Spring, summer

Status: Native

Type: Perennial forb

Identifying characteristics: White showy flower with three petals and yellow stamens. Whorled oval leaves with a tip. Plant height is under two feet tall

Special cautions: The plant may die if leaves are removed. It has a slow growth rate, so it doesn't replenish the plants quickly. This fact can explain its scarcity in some areas with large deer populations. They love the stuff. In fact, you can get a good idea of the deer pressure in an area by noting the abundance—or not—of trillium.

Berries and root, however, are potentially toxic for people. This is another example of why you can't assume a plant is safe just because animals eat it with no ill effects. But perhaps because of the deer, it is endangered in Maine and vulnerable in New York.

Folklore

Trillium is an attractive plant and a nice find in on a hike in the woods. Given its list of common names, you know there are some good stories to be had.

You may find it called a variety of things, including devil's ear, memory root, dragon root, and Indian turnip. After all, something inspired each one though I don't know who Benjamin is.

Trillium is the official flower of Ontario. According to the folklore, it has magical properties. If you wanted to attract a new lover, all you had to do was rub trillium on your naked body, but only on a day when the moon is waxing. And if that doesn't get some attention from the opposite sex, I'm not sure what would.

If there was someone particular you had in mind, you could also attract that person. Just a pinch of the powdered root in her food or drink would make her look favorably on you. For best results, you should do this on a Friday, the day of Venus, when the moon is waxing. This latter use makes me scratch my head, given the fact that the roots are poisonous.

Medicinal Use

The trillium has some of the most curious medicinal uses of the wild plants in this book. The Potawatomi used an infusion of the root as a cure for sore nipples. This is one case where you have to wonder if the cure is worse than the condition.

The concoction is drunk by the inflicted one, then a medicine man pierces the nipples with a dog whisker. Other uses by American Indians include a tea for treating menstrual cramps, which I suppose can hurt as much as a dog whisker on some days. I'll take the cramps.

The settlers had more mundane uses for trillium, though they were diverse. There are accounts of it being used as an expectorant and stimulant. It was also used to treat indigestion, ulcers and insect stings.

Trillium was also known by the moniker, birthroot. It was given to pregnant women for treating a variety of ills, including diseases of the womb and as relief for the pain of childbirth. Herbalists used it to treat irregular menses and cramps. Being a diuretic, it may have offered some relief.

Scientific research has found another potential use for trillium. A study by the University of Mississippi found that it demonstrated significant anti-fungal activity. While the use for sore nipples wasn't confirmed, its purpose may lie elsewhere.

32 TROUT LILY

Common name: Trout lily

Other names: Dog-tooth violet, yellow trout lily, serpent's tongue

Scientific name: *Erythronium americanum*, Lily Family

Habitat: Moist forests

Season: Spring

Status: Native

Type: Perennial forb

Identifying characteristics: Mottled basal leaves. Lily-like white or yellow nodding flower. Plant height is less than one foot tall

Special cautions: Use caution with this one. It may have emetic properties in some individuals. And it's hands off in Iowa where it is listed as threatened.

Folklore

The first thing that may strike you as strange about this plant are the very different common names it is known by. The name, trout lily, refers to the mottled appearance of its basal leaves that resemble a trout. Its leaves are striking, whatever the reference.

The name, dogtooth violet, refers to the appearance of its corm with its dog-like teeth. The name, violet, is a misnomer since it is unrelated to this plant. Anyway, trout lily is more fitting to me.

The moniker, serpent's tongue, is a reference perhaps to the emerging purplish point that makes its appearance in the early spring. Trout lily is one of the earlier spring wildflowers on the scene, well before the trees of the forest have begun to leaf out.

One can imagine many a frightened child running home after a jaunt in the woods after encountering a serpent coming up from underground. It must have made quite the impression.

The trout lily was said to have sprung from the ground where Eve's tears fell when she found out she was pregnant. It is considered the sacred flower of motherhood.

It was also a symbol of the goddesses, Hera and Juno. And like many wild plants, the entire plant of the trout lily was eaten. The leaves and flowers were tasty additions to salads. You could also cook the plant—taking the proper precautions, of course.

Ecology: Bears and deer will both eat the plant.

Medicinal Use

Likewise, the entire plant was used for medicinal purposes. A leaf poultice was used traditionally for treating sores, skin ulcers, and wounds because of its emollient properties. A poultice of the roots was said to remove slivers.

It was also a was a treatment for inflammation and swelling. The Romans were said to grow the plant near their camps to use it for foot sores, so this association goes far back in history.

American Indians used trillium as well. The Iroquois believed it was a contraceptive. Young girls would take the raw plants to prevent getting pregnant. While this use has not been confirmed, scientific evidence shows that trout lily has anti-bacterial properties that support some of its historical uses.

33 VIOLET

Common name: Violet

Other names: Meadow violet, common blue violet, hooded blue violet

Scientific name: *Viola sororia*, Violet Family

Habitat: Rich, moist woods and meadows

Season: Spring

Status: Native

Type: Annual forb

Identifying characteristics: Pale lavender to deep purple leaves with yellow-colored stamens. Leaves are slightly toothed. Plant height is less than one foot tall

Special cautions: And as Terence, the Roman comic dramatist reminds us, "*Moderation in all things.*" The root has emetic properties, especially in large quantities.

Folklore

There are 125 species of violets in the United States. It is the state flower of Illinois, Wisconsin, Rhode Island, and New Jersey.

One of the most interesting of plant legends about violets goes back to the ancient Greeks.

As the story goes, the nymph, Io, was the beloved of Zeus. When Mom Hera found out, she turned her into a white heifer. Io wept at her fate. Zeus was said to have changed her tears into violets. Perhaps for this reason, it is a symbol of constancy in love.

The ancient Italian nobleman, Pliny, wrote of the sweet violet as a way to calm anger and to treat a headache caused by a hangover. There is also mention in the folklore of its ability to clear the mind and to relax the wearer because of its sweet scent. Some even considered it a good luck charm to carry with you at all times. Nicholas Culpepper's 17th century astrological classification of plants mentions an association of violet with the planet, Venus.

The violet has many other stories associated with it. Napoleon Bonaparte was said to have promised to return to France with the blooming of the violets. He did so in March 1815, albeit for a brief time before the Battle of Waterloo. It is considered a herb of good luck for people other than Napoleon.

Some plants have stories associated with them that will certainly leave you wondering, such as the common violet. Legend has it that if you wore a garland of violets around your neck, it could prevent drunkenness. The efficacy of this cure, unfortunately, has been lost in the folklore.

The literature tells us that in addition to these other uses, you could enjoy violets as a food. Its leaves are highly nutritious, providing good sources of vitamins A and C. Violets also contain antioxidants.

They could be added to salads or dried as a pleasant-tasting tea. The flowers were also used then and today as a perfume and as a flavoring syrup or as a candied treat. France makes a delightful liqueur from violets called crème de violette. If you want a proper Aviation cocktail, you need some of this on hand.

From my experience, the violet is the harbinger of morels. When the violets first start appearing, the morels are not far behind. Once the violets cover the forest floor, the morels are done. This observation applies to the Upper Midwest, where violets first appear in the beginning weeks of May.

Medicinal Use

The violet was not used medicinally by American Indians, at least not in the Midwest region that I was able to find. Several nations including the Potawatomi did not even have a name for it.

This account is unusual given the fact that many American Indians could identify 200 to 300 medicinal plants by sight. How violet would escape their notice seems odd. The Cherokee, however, used it for several purposes, including as a spring tonic and a cold and cough remedy, the vitamin C in action here.

The European settlers, on the other hand, used violet extensively, including as a cancer treatment and fever reducer. Its primary use for was treating respiratory issues.

There are accounts of its use as a blood purifier, presumably because bad blood could cause a variety of ailments. Violet has diuretic and analgesic properties so it may have made people more comfortable.

34 VIRGINIA CREEPER

Common name: Virginia creeper

Other names: American ivy, woodbine, five-leaved ivy

Scientific name: *Parthenocissus quinquefolia*, Grape Family

Habitat: Well-drained soils, forests, thickets

Season: Summer

Status: Native

Type: Perennial woody vine

Identifying characteristics: Leaf with five leaflets in star-like shape. Stem is thick and can become woody in older plants

Special cautions: The berries and leaves are toxic. It may also cause dermatitis in some individuals.

Folklore

Virginia creeper is a vigorous and sometimes, tenacious plant, which does make good ground cover. It gets something of a bad rap because it is mistaken for poison ivy. While both can form woody plants, the leaves are different. *"Leaves of three, let it be; Leaves of five, let it thrive."* Thrive is appropriate in this case. The plant makes a good addition to the urban garden where it can tolerate smoke and other irritants.

Though it was eaten by some American Indians such as the Montana, the Iroquois considered it a poison, perhaps with good reason. The fruit has some sweetness to it, though the small size of the berries makes the effort hardly worth the trouble.

As one may expect with a plant with berries, Virginia creeper was used a dye by the Kiowa people for the skin and for feathers in war dances.

Food: Stem-sugar syrup

Ecology: Cover and food for birds; minor value to mammals

Medicinal Use

To be clear, some individuals may experience contact dermatitis caused by the needle-like crystals in the plant. And, the berries contain oxalic acid. These are good reasons to use Virginia creeper with caution.

Nevertheless, the association with poison ivy exists, but not like you think. Some used a wash made with the plant to treat its nasty itch as kind of an odd twist on its unfortunate association.

Virginia creeper's resemblance to poison ivy is ironic given the fact that the Iroquois used it as a cure for poison sumac, another plant that causes contact dermatitis. It was used to treat swelling and wounds as well.

Herbalists considered Virginia creeper as a general tonic and expectorant. There are accounts of it being used to treat dropsy, an old term that describes swelling in the soft tissues.

Given these uses, it's interesting to note that Virginia creeper acted as something of a cure during the Great Plague of London. It helped induce perspiration, bolstered by its antiseptic qualities.

In addition to these uses, early herbalists used it with some success against headaches of different sorts. If you could just get past the bitter taste and purgative properties . . .

While some of its historical uses have yet to be discovered, a study by the Chinese Academy of Medical Sciences and Peking Union Medical College found that Virginia creeper contains resveratrol. This substance has received a great deal of attention in the scientific community because of its possible potential to improve cardiovascular health. It has also shown antioxidant and anti-inflammatory properties.

35 WILD BERGAMOT

Common name: Wild Bergamot

Other names: Bee balm, wild oregano, horse mint

Scientific name: *Monarda fistulosa* Mint Family

Habitat: Dry to wet prairies, woods and fields

Season: Spring through fall

Status: Native

Type: Perennial forb

Identifying characteristics: Tubular pinkish-lavender blooms

Special cautions: It is considered historical in Rhode Island. You might want to pass on collecting it there. And because it's attractive to bees, please be careful when collecting or even just being in the area of wild bergamot.

Folklore

Bergamot has both culinary and medicinal uses. It stands unique in that it is the only plant indigenous to North America that contains thymol. Thymol has a long history of use going back to the ancient Egyptians who used it to preserve mummies.

The literature also mentions its use in book and paper conservation, following along those lines. And it seems as if these were good uses for it. Bergamot's anti-microbial properties and pesticide qualities certainly would have made it a good choice for these uses.

Bergamot is a very aromatic plant that can make a delightful tea from the leaves. You can also add the leaves to a salad for an addition that is high in vitamins A and C. However, this is not the same as bergamot essential oil like in Earl Grey tea.

This bergamot tea was the drink of choice after the Boston Tea Party when colonists protested the high taxes imposed on tea. It was also known as Oswego tea during the time of the Revolution.

It lends itself well as a flavoring to foods. When I first encountered bergamot, my immediate thought was the pizza plant. The strong scent resembles oregano. That was the local name for the plant, in a nod to its other common name, wild oregano. Given that both oregano and bergamot are in the Mint Family, the association probably wasn't too far off.

Ecology: As you might guess from its other common names, bergamot is of special value to bees as well as hummingbirds.

Medicinal Use

Bergamot was used by both the settlers and the American Indians. Like some other plants, it served a host of purposes. It treated the common complaints of digestive issues, which you might expect being in the Mint Family. Mints work by relaxing muscles of the digestive tract.

Herbalists also used it to treat respiratory conditions. It was even used as an inhalant for the latter. The Ojibwa used it in a similar fashion.

The leaves were also used in a poultice for treating sores, skin problems, and headaches. It was said to be something of a cure-all, with its anti-bacterial and anti-fungus properties. It was even used to treat intestinal worms and nose bleeds.

Bergamot treated many ills. Some used a tea for treating gingivitis. That's not as far-fetched as it sounds because bergamot contains a naturally-occurring antiseptic called thymol. This chemical lent itself to modern uses.

Manufacturers used thymol in many common products, including cigarettes as well as treatments for intestinal worms. It was even used as body wash historically, with the added benefit of being an insect repellent. Thymol is a non-persisting pesticide, making it an effective treatment.

Its use for treating skin conditions has been confirmed scientifically from findings of a study by the Belgorod State University in Russia. Researchers found that bergamot essential oil possessed anti-bacterial and anti-inflammatory properties. They also found it effective for treating seborrhea, a common cause of acne.

36 WILD GINGER

Common name: Wild Ginger

Other names: Canadian wildginger, sturgeon potato, coltsfoot

Scientific name: *Asarum canadense*, Birthwort Family

Habitat: Woodlands

Season: Spring, summer

Status: Native

Type: Perennial forb

Identifying characteristics: Thick fleshy heart-shaped leaves, usually found in small clusters. The red flower is at the base of the plant and easily missed. Plant height is under one foot tall

Special cautions: The leaves may cause skin irritation in some people. The flowers and stem may be toxic. Pregnant women should not consume wild ginger. It's off limits in Maine where it is threatened.

Folklore

Wild ginger is a striking plant. It is low growing, forming attractive mats in moist, shady areas. You might even find it at your local garden center as a nice addition for the shade garden. However, there is a downside. Since insects, namely, flies, pollinate it, its odor may lessen its appeal.

As you might expect, the root of wild ginger was used as a flavoring agents by American Indians, which was eventually adopted by the settlers. It was often added to foods to make them palatable.

And like commercially-grown ginger, it was a welcome digestive cure. It was given to individuals with a weak stomach to get them to eat. However, the taste is not an exact substitute for the ginger you buy at the grocery store even if the effect was similar.

Wild ginger appears early in the spring. Its foliage make it one of the more elegant of the spring wildflowers. The aromatic nature of wild ginger root makes it an effective insect repellent when burned as an incense. The Chippewa would roast the roots and then sprinkle them on their clothes as a sort of perfume.

As an example of the Doctrine of Signatures, the bumpy surface of wild ginger may explain the early belief that it was used by witches to remove their warts. There's no word on whether it helped or not.

The Iroquois had similar associations, using an infusion to remove ghost contamination and to prevent bad dreams caused by the dead. They also used it as a stimulant against laziness, perhaps caused by the evil spirits.

Medicinal Use

Settlers used ginger as you might today for treating digestive issues. It was also used to treat colds and sores. A tea made from ginger was a tonic for the heart. The early settlers called it Canada snakeroot and used it to treat fevers. The literature makes mention of its use as a cure for deafness as well.

The Menominee and Ojibwa had a very different use for ginger that is worth noting. There was a belief that a person in a weakened state or one with an upset stomach should not eat whatever it was that he craved.

He could eat whatever he wanted, however, if he chewed or ate a bit of the root. This use for stomach problems is widespread among the different peoples.

Ginger was a common treatment for swelling and inflammation wherever it occurred on the body. The Cherokee even used it to treat swollen breasts. They also used ginger as a female tonic to stimulate menstruation.

Many cultures used it for treating colds, coughs, and fevers. Some, such as the Chippewa, added ginger to other medicines to strengthen their effects. Given its digestive and anti-inflammatory effects, it seems fitting that herbalists would use ginger as a general cure.

While not studied as extensively as other species in its genus, wild ginger has shown antibacterial activity, which can explains its use for treating sores and fevers. It has also been found to contain antioxidants called flavonoids.

37 WILD ROSE

Common name: Wild Rose

Other names: Prairie rose, wild rose, dwarf prairie rose

Scientific name: *Rosa arkansana*, Rose Family

Habitat: Prairies and meadows

Season: Summer

Status: Native

Type: Perennial subshrub

Identifying characteristics: Low-growing shrub with showy flowers

Special cautions: This plant has thorns and little hairs beneath the flesh of the fruit which may prove irritating. Alas, you may not find it in Ohio as it is presumed extirpated.

Folklore

There are over 100 species of rose in North America and over 10,000 species in cultivation. The prairie rose is one of the native varieties. It is not the same plant as the hateful and invasive multi-flora rose, an invasive plant. Even the deer won't have anything to do with that one.

It is the state flower of Iowa and North Dakota. We've had a long love affair with these flowers through the ages. Roses have been admired and cultivated for over 2,000 years.

The rose was revered by the ancient Greeks and Romans, the legend saying that it sprung from the blood of Adonis, a Phoenician demi-god of beauty and desire in Greek mythology. The rose has a strong association with all matters of the heart. It was sacred to both the Greek and Roman gods of love, Eros and Cupid, respectively.

Success was yours if you were fortunate enough to dream about roses. However, the roses must be red. If you dream of black roses, evil was afoot. If you wanted to know who your future husband was to be, all you had to do was sleep with a rose that you picked on Midsummer's Eve between your breasts. Watch out for the thorns!

Roses, in general, have a wide assortment of magical associations in the folklore, primarily on the positive side. It is linked with psychic powers and healing. It was also said to a plant for luck and protection.

Some of these uses involve the conjuring of fairies, which you could do by planting roses in your garden. The Slavic peoples believed that wild roses could keep vampires at bay.

Both settlers and American Indians ate the hips, flowers, leaves, and shoots of the prairie rose. Some cultures, such as the Pawnee and Omaha, smoked the inner bark, either alone or with tobacco.

The hips, of course, are high in vitamins C, E, and A as well as magnesium and calcium, making the rose a nutritious plant. Its vitamin C content, for example, is seven times the daily allowance.

The leaves were added to soups and stews for flavoring. There were also made into jams and dried for tea. Nevertheless, the Dakota considered the hips a starvation food to be eaten during times of famine.

You'll likely see other uses of roses of other varieties. They include the syrup of red rose, official in the United States Pharmacopceia as well as French liqueurs distilled from the petals.

Ecology: Special value to native bees

Medicinal Use

The high vitamin C content made the wild rose something of a spring tonic. The Chippewa used a decoction of root as a stimulant. It was also used for treating bleeding wounds and sore eyes. The Pawnee used it in a poultice for treating burns.

Rose has astringent properties and makes a good skin care wash. It has anti-inflammatory and aromatic properties. Its nutritional value may explain its use as a heart tonic and perhaps its association with blood. Its vitamin K content is essential for clotting of blood.

38 YARROW

Common name: Yarrow

Other names: Bloodwort, milfoil, carpenter's weed, common yarrow, devil's nettle, thousand leaf, devil's plaything, wound wort

Scientific name: *Achillea millefolium*, Aster Family

Habitat: Moist to wet fields, roadsides, disturbed sites

Season: Spring through fall

Status: Native and introduced

Type: Perennial forb

Identifying characteristics: White flower head, with lace-like leaves. Aromatic when crushed.

Special cautions: Yarrow may cause dermatitis in some individuals. The literature does not recommended yarrow for long-term use because of possible toxicity. There are accounts of it being used to induce abortions. Pregnant women, therefore, should avoid it. While abundant elsewhere, it is considered of special concern in Maine.

Folklore

Whether it is because of its medicinal values or other associations, yarrow is found throughout North America in all 50 states, including Canada. It has several culinary uses, one of which you may surmise by its moniker, old man's pepper.

Yarrow is an aromatic plant used as a salad green or a tea from the dried leaves. The people of Orkney Island thought that the tea could dispel melancholy. It was said that yarrow made a more potent beer than hops, which may explain why it chases the blues away.

Yarrow is a plant brimming with legends. It was said to be a love medicine. If you wanted to know who your future husband or wife was, all you had to do was gather some yarrow, sew it up in flannel and place it under your pillow on Beltane Eve (April 30) or on a night with a new moon. Other stories are not as innocent.

It was said that Satan and witches used it to caste spells and that it may have been dedicated to the devil. With names like devil's plaything, devil's nettle, and bad man's plaything, you may question having it around your garden. It wasn't all bad though. The Potawatomi, on the other hand, used the flowers smudged on coals to ward off evil spirits.

An old wives tale offers a similar use. Legend has it that if you sprinkled yarrow on your doorstep, the devil would not enter your home. It also has an association with the planet, Venus, based on Nicholas Culpepper's 17th century astrological classification of plants. It was said to have other magical associations with psychic powers and exorcism. One legend says that yarrow could help you find out if your lover was true to you.

Ecology: Yarrow attracts predatory insects that feed on pests such as flies and ants, making it of special value to native bees—and humans. It can become weedy and invasive. Important food source for deer.

Medicinal Use

Legend has it that yarrow's genus name, *Achillea,* comes from the story of Achilles, who was said to have used this plant to treat the wounds of his soldiers during the battle at Troy, prompting its name in the field, "*herbal militaris.*" The story must have stuck. Early settlers used it similarly for stopping blood flow.

This property led to its uses for other related issues, such as hemorrhages and nosebleeds. It would seem that its uses associated with bleeding and hemorrhages may indeed have been a good course of treatment. Over 100 biologically-active compounds have been identified in yarrow, leaving the possibility open for more medicinal uses.

There are numerous accounts of yarrow being used to treat a variety of skin conditions, from snakebites to poison ivy to bruises. A poultice was used for treating headaches and skin rashes. Yarrow has antibiotic and analgesic properties that can account for these uses. There are even accounts of it being a cure for hair loss.

Many American Indian nations revered yarrow, calling it the *"life medicine."* Yarrow was also used to treat disorders of the reproductive and gastrointestinal systems because of its effects on the mucous membranes. Some cultures, such as the Clallam, used it during childbirth. It was said to hurry up the baby and help expel the afterbirth. Others, including the Iroquois, viewed yarrow as a panacea for treating any kind of illness.

Some American Indians used yarrow as an inhalant. The Potawatomi's use was a two-part cure that began with driving out the evil spirits causing the illness. Its scent was then believed to revive a person in a coma. Whatever type of pain you had from toothache to burns to broken bones, yarrow was the cure of choice. The literature also contains several references to its use for a variety of respiratory conditions, including colds.

Scientific research has yielded compelling that supports many of its traditional uses. A study by the Universidade Paranaense in Brazil confirmed that yarrow does indeed have pain-relieving properties, which explains many of the folklore remedies using it.

In addition, it has been shown to have protective effects for the cardiovascular system. A study by the Università degli Studi di Padova in Italy found that it can reduce vascular inflammation. These findings support other research by the Universidade Federal do Paraná in Brazil, which found that yarrow has hypotensive properties, meaning that it may help lower blood pressure.

39 THE LAST WORD

Final Thoughts

What a journey! I could have included so many more plants, all with equally interesting stories, uses, and legends. I can't help feeling that the world must have been a scary place back in the day, with all these "cures" for witches, devils, and all sorts of evil forces. Now, we have pollution, climate change, and rising oceans to contend with.

The plants and their folklore give us unique insights into the world that existed before today. We know more about the challenges that people faced, as well as their fears. The unknown, apparently, was something that left many feeling uncomfortable and in search of a cure.

Even their names tell us volumes about the world before us: ghost plant, serpent's tongue, and devil's guts. Be glad for supermarkets and farmer's markets and all those people in the field who stand up for the weeds and cursed plants! Because of them, you can enjoy purslane, dandelion, and other botanical treasures. Bon appetit!

BIBLIOGRAPHY

Alternative Nature Herbals. "Angelica Herb." Accessed June 17, 2014. http://www.altnature.com/gallery/angelica.htm.

American Botanical Council. "News Release." May 7, 2010. Accessed June 17, 2014. http://abc.herbalgram.org/

Annie's Remedy Essential Oils & Herbs. "Annies Remedy." Accessed June 17, 2014. http://www.anniesremedy.com/.

Baretta, Irinéia Paulina, Regiane Américo Felizardo, Vanessa Fávero Bimbato, Maísa Gonçalves Jorge Dos Santos, Candida Aparecida Leite Kassuya, Arquimedes Gasparotto Junior, and Roberto . . . Andreatini. "Anxiolytic-like Effects of Acute and Chronic Treatment with Achillea Millefolium L. Extract." *Journal of Ethnopharmacology* 140, no. 1 (2012): 46-54. doi:10.1016/j.jep.2011.11.047.

Birkett, Michael A., Ahmed Hassanali, Solveig Hoglund, Jan Pettersson, and John A. Pickett. "Repellent Activity of Catmint, Nepeta Cataria, and Iridoid Nepetalactone Isomers against Afro-tropical Mosquitoes, Ixodid Ticks and Red Poultry Mites." *Phytochemistry* 72, no. 1 (2011): 109-14. doi:10.1016/j.phytochem.2010.09.016.

Bisht, D. S., S. C. Joschi, R. C. Padalia, and C. S. Mathela. "Isoiridomyrmecin Rich Essential Oil from Nepeta Erecta Benth. and Its Antioxidant Activity." *Natural Product Research* 26, no. 1 (2012): 29-35. doi:dx.doi.org/10.1080/14786419.2010.531393.

The Celtic Connection. "A Witches' Herbal Reference." Accessed June 25, 2014. http://wicca.com/celtic/herbal/magickal0.htm.

Cienki, John J., and Larry Zaret. "An Internet Misadventure: Bloodroot Salve Toxicity." *The Journal of Alternative and Complementary Medicine* 16, no. 10 (2010): 1125-127. doi:10.1089/acm.2010.0140.

Culpeper, Nicholas. *Culpeper's Complete Herbal: Consisting of a Comprehensive Description of Nearly All Herbs with Their Medicinal Properties and Directions for Compounding the Medicines Extracted from Them.* London: W. Foulsham, 1923.

Cybulska, Paulina, Sidharath D. Thakur, Brian C. Foster, Ian M. Scott, Renée I. Leduc, John T. Arnason, and Jo-Anne R. Dillon. "Extracts of Canadian First Nations Medicinal Plants, Used as Natural Products, Inhibit Neisseria Gonorrhoeae Isolates With Different Antibiotic Resistance Profiles." *Sexually Transmitted Diseases* 38, no. 7 (2011): 667-71. doi:10.1097/OLQ.0b013e31820cb166.

Dall'Acqua, Stefano, Chiara Bolego, Andrea Cignarella, Rosa Maria Gaion, and Gabbriella Innocenti. "Vasoprotective Activity of Standardized Achillea Millefolium Extract." *Phytomedicine* 18, no. 12 (2011): 1031-036. doi:10.1016/j.phymed.2011.05.005.

Duke, James A. "Dr. Duke's Phytochemical and Ethnobotanical Databases." Accessed June 25, 2014. http://www.ars-grin.gov/cgi-bin/duke/ethnobot.pl?Angelica%20atropurpurea.

Durzan, Don J. "Arginine, Scurvy and Cartier's "tree of Life"" *Journal of Ethnobiology and Ethnomedicine* 5, no. 1 (2009): 5. doi:10.1186/1746-4269-5-5.

Escobar, Franco Matías, María Carola Sabini, Silvia Matilde Zanon, Carlos Eugenio Tonn, and Liliana Inés Sabini. "Antiviral Effect and Mode of Action of Methanolic Extract OfL. on Pseudorabies Virus (strain RC/79)." *Natural Product Research*, 2011, 1-5. doi:10.1080/14786419.2011.576394.

Foster, Steven, and James A. Duke. *A Field Guide to Medicinal Plants: Eastern and Central North America.* Boston: Houghton Mifflin, 1998.

Foster, Steven. "Steven Foster Group, Inc." 2011. Accessed June 25, 2014. http://www.stevenfoster.com/education/monograph/echinacea1.html.

Gazzani, Gabriella, Maria Daglia, and Adele Papetti. "Food Components with Anticaries Activity." *Current Opinion in Biotechnology* 23, no. 2 (2012): 153-59. doi:10.1016/j.copbio.2011.09.003.

Gescher, Kirsten, and Alexandra M. Deters. "Typha Latifolia L. Fruit Polysaccharides Induce the Differentiation and Stimulate the Proliferation of Human Keratinocytes in Vitro." *Journal of Ethnopharmacology* 137, no. 1 (2011): 352-58. doi:10.1016/j.jep.2011.05.042.

Hufford, Charles D., Shihchih Liu, and Alice M. Clark. "Antifungal Activity of Trillium Grandiflorum Constituents." *Journal of Natural Products* 51, no. 1 (1988): 94-98. doi:10.1021/np50055a013.

Iwashina, Tsukasa, and Junichi Kitajima. "Chalcone and Flavonol Glycosides from Asarum Canadense (Aristolochiaceae)." *Phytochemistry* 55, no. 8 (2000): 971-74. doi:10.1016/S0031-9422(00)00216-8.

Jasuja, Reema, Freda H. Passam, Daniel R. Kennedy, Sarah H. Kim, Lotte Van Hessem, Lin Lin, Sheryl R. Bowley, and Robert & . . . Flaumenhaft. "Protein Disulfide Isomerase Inhibitors Constitute a New Class of Antithrombotic Agents." *Journal of Clinical Investigation* 122, no. 6 (2012): 2104-113. doi:10.1172/JCI61228.

Jensen, A. N., H. Mejer, L. Mølbak, M. Langkjær, T. K. Jensen, Ø. Angen, T. Martinussen, and A. & . . . Roepstorff. "The Effect of a Diet with Fructan-rich Chicory Roots on Intestinal Helminths and Microbiota with Special Focus on Bifidobacteria and Campylobacter in Piglets around Weaning." *Animal* 5, no. 06 (2011): 851-60. doi:10.1017/S175173111000251X.

Kim, Jinpyo, Seokbean Song, Iksoo Lee, Youngho Kim, Ickdong Yoo, Inja Ryoo, and Kihwan Bae. "Anti-inflammatory Activity of Constituents from Glechoma Hederacea Var. Longituba." *Bioorganic & Medicinal Chemistry Letters* 21, no. 11 (2011): 3483-487. doi:10.1016/j.bmcl.2011.02.002.

Kováts, Nora, András Ács, Flóra Gölöncsér, and Anikó Barabás. "Quantifying of Bactericide Properties of Medicinal Plants." *Plant Signaling & Behavior* 6, no. 6 (2011): 777-79. doi:10.4161/psb.6.6.15356.

"Lady Bird Johnson Wildflower Center - The University of Texas at Austin." Accessed June 25, 2014. http://www.wildflower.org/.

Lu, Yinrong, and L. Yeap Foo. "Constitution of Some Chemical Components of Apple Seed." *Food Chemistry* 61, no. 1-2 (1998): 29-33. doi:10.1016/S0308-8146(97)00123-4.

Mccarthy, Eibhlín, and Jim M. O'mahony. "What's in a Name? Can Mullein Weed Beat TB Where Modern Drugs Are Failing?" *Evidence-Based Complementary and Alternative Medicine* 2011 (2011): 1-7. doi:10.1155/2011/239237.

Medscape. "Scurvy ." March 21, 2013. Accessed May 28, 2014. http://emedicine.medscape.com/article/125350-overview.

Mikkelson, Barbara, and David P. Mikkelson. "Snopes.com: Apple Seeds and Cyanide." February 20, 2007. Accessed June 25, 2014. http://www.snopes.com/food/warnings/apples.asp.

Milovanovic, M., D. Zivkovic, and B. Vucelic-Radovic. "Antioxidant Effects of Glechoma Hederacea as a Food Additive." *Natural Product Communications* 5, no. 1 (2010): 61-63.

Moraes, R. M., H. Lata, E. Bedir, M. Maqbool, and K. Cushman. "The American Mayapple and Its Potential for Podophyllotoxin Production." In *Trends in New Crops and New Uses*, edited by J. Janick and A. Whipkey, 527-32. Alexandria, VA: ASHS Press, 2002.

Obiang-Obounou, Brice W., Ok-Hwa Kang, Jang-Gi Choi, Joon-Ho Keum, Sung-Bae Kim, Su-Hyun Mun, Dong-Won Shin, and Dong-Yeul & . . . Kwon. "The Mechanism of Action of Sanguinarine against Methicillin-resistant Staphylococcus Aureus." *The Journal of Toxicological Sciences* 36, no. 3 (2011): 277-83. doi:10.2131/jts.36.277.

Ohio State University Extension. "Ohio Perennial and Biennial Weed Guide." Accessed June 25, 2014. http://www.oardc.ohio-state.edu/weedguide/singlerecord.asp?id=880.

Plants For A Future. "Plants For A Future." 2012. http://www.pfaf.org/.

Ray, L. "Podophyllum Peltatum and Observations on the Creek and Cherokee Indians: William Bartram's Preservation of Native American Pharmacology." *Yale Journal of Biology and Medicine* 82, no. 1 (2009): 25-36.

Salama, Rima. "Identification and Evaluation of Agents Isolated from Traditionally Used Herbs against Ophiophagus Hannah Venom." *Drug Discoveries & Therapeutics* 6, no. 1 (2012): 18-23. doi:10.5582/ddt.2012.v6.1.18.

Shukla, Y.n, Anil Srivastava, Sunil Kumar, and Sushil Kumar. "Phytotoxic and Antimicrobial Constituents of Argyreia Speciosa and Oenothera Biennis." *Journal of Ethnopharmacology* 67, no. 2 (1999): 241-45. doi:10.1016/S0378-8741(99)00017-3.

Slavokhotova, Anna A., Tatyana I. Odintsova, Eugene A. Rogozhin, Alexander K. Musolyamov, Yaroslav A. Andreev, Eugene V. Grishin, and Tsezi A. Egorov. "Isolation, Molecular Cloning and Antimicrobial Activity of Novel Defensins from Common Chickweed (Stellaria Media L.) Seeds." *Biochimie* 93, no. 3 (2011): 450-56. doi:10.1016/j.biochi.2010.10.019.

Smirnova, G., Z. Samoilova, N. Muzyka, and O. Oktyabrsky. "Influence of Plant Polyphenols and Medicinal Plant Extracts on Antibiotic Susceptibility of Escherichia Coli." *Journal of Applied Microbiology* 113, no. 1 (2012): 192-99. doi:10.1111/j.1365-2672.2012.05322.x.

Smith, Huron H. Selections from Ethnobotany of the Menomini Indians. S.l.: S.n., 1923.

Southwest Colorado Wildflowers. "Leucanthemum Vulgare." Accessed June 25, 2014. H://www.swcoloradowildflowers.com

Souza, Priscila De, Arquimedes Gasparotto, Sandra Crestani, Maria Élida Alves Stefanello, Maria Consuelo Andrade Marques, José Eduardo Da Silva-Santos, and Cândida Aparecida Leite Kassuya. "Hypotensive Mechanism of the Extracts and Artemetin Isolated from Achillea Millefolium L. (Asteraceae) in Rats." *Phytomedicine* 18, no. 10 (2011): 819-25. doi:10.1016/j.phymed.2011.02.005.

Starr Dana, Mrs. William. *How to Know the Wild Flowers*. Boston, MA: Houghton Mifflin Company, 1989.

Stewart, Amy. *The Drunken Botanist: The Plants That Create the World's Great Drinks*. Chapel Hill, NC: Algonquin Books of Chapel Hill, 2013.

Tang, Xu-Dong, Xin Zhou, and Ke-Yuan Zhou. "Dauricine Inhibits Insulin-like Growth Factor-I-induced Hypoxia Inducible Factor 1α Protein Accumulation and Vascular Endothelial Growth Factor Expression in Human Breast Cancer Cells." *Acta Pharmacologica Sinica* 30, no. 5 (2009): 605-16. doi:10.1038/aps.2009.8.

Tokuda, H., H. Ohigashi, K. Koshimizu, and Y. Ito. "Inhibitory Effects of Ursolic and Oleanolic Acid on Skin Tumor Promotion by 12-O-tetradecanoylphorbol-13-acetate." *Cancer Letters* 33, no. 3 (1986): 279-85. http://www.ncbi.nlm.nih.gov/pubmed/3802058.

University of Michigan. "Native American Ethnobotany." 2012. Accessed June 25, 2014. http://herb.umd.umich.edu/.

University of Wisconsin-Stevens Point. "University of Wisconsin-Stevens Point Freckmann Herbarium." Accessed June 25, 2014. http://wisplants.uwsp.edu/.

U.S. Forest Service. "Medicinal Botany." 2011. Accessed June 25, 2014. http://www.fs.fed.us/wildflowers/ethnobotany/medicinal/index.shtml. U.S. Geological Survey. "Northeast Wetland Flora." 2006. Accessed June 25, 2014. http://www.npwrc.usgs.gov/

USDA Natural Resources Conservation Service. (n.d.). Eastern Purple Coneflower. Retrieved from Http://plants.usda.gov/factsheet/pdf/fs_ecpu.pdf

USDA Natural Resources Conservation Service. "Welcome to the PLANTS Database | USDA PLANTS." Accessed June 25, 2014. http://plants.usda.gov/java/.

Virginia Tech Weed Identification Guide. "Common Mullein: Verbascum Thapsus." Accessed June 25, 2014. http://www.ppws.vt.edu/scott/weed_id/vesth.htm.

Vrchovská, V., J. Spilková, P. Valentão, C. Sousa, P. B. Andrade, and R. M. Seabra. "Assessing the Antioxidative Properties and Chemical Composition Ofinfusion." *Natural Product Research* 22, no. 9 (2008): 735-46. doi:10.1080/14786410601132360.

Wegiera, M., H. D. Smolarz, M. Jedruch, M. Korczak, and K. Koproń. "Cytotoxic Effect of Some Medicinal Plants from Asteraceae Family on J-45.01 Leukemic Cell Line--pilot Study." *Acta Poloniae Pharmaceutica* 69, no. 2 (2012): 263-68.

WholeHealthMD. "Dandelion." July 21, 2011. Accessed June 17, 2014. http://wholehealthmd.com.

WholeHealthMD. "Echinacea." July 28, 2010. Accessed June 17, 2014. http://www.wholehealthmd.com.

WholeHealthMD. "Quercetin." May 7, 2010. Accessed June 17, 2014. http://www.wholehealthmd.com.

WholeHealthMD. "Resveratrol." September 24, 2008. Accessed June 17, 2014. http://www.wholehealthmd.com.

Yang, Ting, Feng Luo, Yongchun Shen, Jing An, Xiaoou Li, Xinyu Liu, Binwu Ying, and Fuqiang & . . . Wen. "Quercetin Attenuates Airway Inflammation and Mucus Production Induced by Cigarette Smoke in Rats."

International Immunopharmacology 13, no. 1 (2012): 73-81. doi:10.1016/j.intimp.2012.03.006.

Yang, Zhengfeng, Chenghai Li, Xiu Wang, Chunyan Zhai, Zhengfang Yi, Lei Wang, Bisheng Liu, and Jian & . . . Luo. "Dauricine Induces Apoptosis, Inhibits Proliferation and Invasion through Inhibiting NF-κB Signaling Pathway in Colon Cancer Cells." *Journal of Cellular Physiology* 225, no. 1 (2010): 266-75. doi:10.1002/jcp.22261.

Young, Harry, Janine M. Gilbert, Shona H. Murray, and Roderick D. Ball. "Causal Effects of Aroma Compounds on Royal Gala Apple Flavours." *Journal of the Science of Food and Agriculture* 71, no. 3 (1996): 329-36. doi:10.1002/(SICI)1097-0010(199607)71:33.3.CO;2-#.

Zaini, Rana G., Kirsten Brandt, Malcolm R. Clench, and Christine L. Le Maitre. "Effects of Bioactive Compounds from Carrots (Daucus Carota L.), Polyacetylenes, Beta-Carotene and Lutein on Human Lymphoid Leukaemia Cells." *Anti-Cancer Agents in Medicinal Chemistry* 12, no. 6 (2012): 640-52. doi:10.2174/187152012800617704.

Zaini, Rana, Malcolm R. Clench, and Christine L. Le Maitre. "Bioactive Chemicals from Carrot (Juice Extracts for the Treatment of Leukemia." *Journal of Medicinal Food* 14, no. 11 (2011): 1303-312. doi:10.1089/jmf.2010.0284.

Zhilyakova, E. T., O. O. Novikov, E. N. Naumenko, L. V. Krichkovskaya, T. S. Kiseleva, E. Yu. Timoshenko, M. Yu. Novikova, and S. A. Litvinov. "Study of Monarda Fistulosa Essential Oil as a Prospective Antiseborrheic Agent." *Bulletin of Experimental Biology and Medicine* 148, no. 4 (2009): 612-14. doi:10.1007/s10517-010-0777-7.

IMAGE CREDITS

Angelica: Robert H. Mohlenbrock. USDA NRCS. 1995. Northeast wetland flora: Field office guide to plant species. Northeast National Technical Center, Chester. Courtesy of USDA NRCS Wetland Science Institute.

Aster: Jennifer Anderson @ USDA-NRCS PLANTS Database

Bloodroot: Jennifer Anderson. United States, IA, Muscatine Co., Muscatine, Wild Cat Den State Park. 2000.

Butter and eggs: Dendroica cerulea @ Flickr

Catnip: Saucy Salad @ Flickr

Chickweed: Jennifer Anderson. United States, IA, Scott Co., Davenport, Nahant Marsh. 2002.

Cinquefoil: Jennifer Anderson. United States, IA, Jackson Co., McNeil Preserve. 2002.

Columbine: Jennifer Anderson. United States, IA, Jackson Co., Eden Valley Refuge. 2002.

Creeping Charlie: JacobEnos @ Flickr

Evening primrose: Charles de Martigny @ Flickr

Indian pipe: Muffet @ Flickr

May apple: Jennifer Anderson @ USDA-NRCS PLANTS Database

Pussy toes: Joshua Mayer @ Flickr

Spiderwort: Ria Hills @ stock.xchng

Sweet flag: Jack Greenlee @ U.S. Forest Service

Virginia creeper: Robert H. Mohlenbrock @ USDA-NRCS PLANTS Database / USDA SCS. 1991. Southern wetland flora: Field office guide to plant species. South National Technical Center, Fort Worth.

Wild bergamot: Robert H. Mohlenbrock @ USDA-NRCS PLANTS Database / USDA NRCS. 1992. Western wetland flora: Field office guide to plant species. West Region, Sacramento.

Wild ginger: Jennifer Anderson @ USDA-NRCS PLANTS Database

Wild rose: jumpinjimmyjava @ Flickr

All other images are in the public domain or my own unless otherwise noted.

ABOUT THE AUTHOR

Chris Dinesen Rogers was born in suburban Chicago. Acting on her love of the outdoors and conservation, she volunteered with Brookfield Zoo and the Illinois Department of Natural Resources. In 1988, She moved to Minnesota to pursue a career in natural resources.

Chris has worked with the U.S. Forest Service, U.S. Fish and Wildlife Service, and the Nature Conservancy. She and her husband, Norm, continued volunteering for environmental causes with the National Park Service at Mammoth Cave National Park in Kentucky. In 2000, both Chris and Norm were awarded the state of Kentucky Colonel award for their work in restoring parts of Mammoth Cave.

She taught at both the community college and university level. In 2002, she began her own art business. Creativity continues to be a driving force with Chris. She started freelance writing and continues to promote conservation and health education.

Other Works by the Author:
101 Things to Do on the Wisconsin Great River Road
How to Achieve Your Fitness and Wellness Potential
101 Tips for the Adventurous Cook
Murder to Order